BEGINNING CONTEMPLATIVE PRAYER

BEGINNING CONTEMPLATIVE PRAYER

Out of Chaos Into Quiet

Sr. Kathryn Hermes, FSP

PUBLISHED BY ST. ANTHONY MESSENGER PRESS
CINCINNATI, OHIO

Published by St. Anthony Messenger Press
28 W. Liberty St.
Cincinnati, OH 45202
www.servantbooks.com
Cover design by Paul Higdon - Minneapolis, MN

04 10 9 8 7 6 5 4

Printed in the United States of America
ISBN 1-56955-269-X

DEDICATION

To Sr. Thomas Halpin, FSP
from whom I have learned the fidelity of God

CONTENTS

Acknowledgments / 9

Introduction / 11

Part I. Encounter: The Rhythm Begins / 15

1. Cultivate Stillness and Silence / 17
2. Live Gently on the Earth / 23
3. Invite God to Come Near / 29
4. Prepare to Ascend the Heights / 37

Part II. Engagement: The Practice of Prayer / 41

5. Remain in God's Presence: Lessons From the Life of Brother Lawrence / 45
6. Let the Spirit Direct You: Lessons From the Life of St. Ignatius of Loyola / 51
7. Experience the Longing to Touch God: Lessons From *Lectio Divina* / 61
8. Simply Love: Lessons From *The Cloud of Unknowing* / 71
9. Called to the Feast: Lessons From the Life of Venerable James Alberione / 79
10. Wrapped in the Heart of God: Lessons From the Life of Simone Weil / 89
11. The Courtesy of God: Lessons From the Life of Blessed Julian of Norwich / 95

Part III. Commitment: The Total Gift / 103

12. Commit to Living Freely / 105
13. Commit to Reconciliation / 109
14. Commit to Carrying Christ's Cross / 115
15. Commit in the Dark Nights / 121

Part IV. Perseverance: Prelude to Transformation / 129

16. Keep Walking / 133
17. Practice a Life of Prayer / 137
18. Obtain Spiritual Direction / 141
19. Tell What You Have Seen / 149

Bibliography / 153

ACKNOWLEDGMENTS

A religious writes from within a community, and the pages of this book spring from the Pauline heritage that I have been privileged to share with so many other Daughters of St. Paul. Therefore the first persons I wish to acknowledge with gratitude are the sisters with whom I have shared my life and my prayer for the past twenty-two years. Without them and our Pauline spiritual tradition, these pages would never have come to be.

In a special way I thank Sr. Germana Santos, FSP. Her belief that I could write helped me over the first panic an author has when he or she faces an empty page. Sr. Thomas Halpin, FSP and Sr. Virginia H. Richards, FSP should be co-authors with me. They have taught me so much about prayer, suffering, and love. Both of them helped weave these pages into a book, and their thoughts are as present here as my own. I thank Br. Romeo Bonsaint, SC; Carol Fitzpatick; Sr. Mary Lea Hill, FSP; Fr. Emmanuel Sullivan, O.C.D.; and Fr. Joseph H. Casey, S.J. for reading through various sets of drafts.

Finally, I am deeply grateful to my parents, who read and edited the book three times. They were my first teachers of prayer, and evidently, from the extensive comments on the drafts, they still hold that position. Thanks.

INTRODUCTION

Our Catholic tradition is one of mysticism and passion, of spiritual journeys and pilgrimages, of worship and prayer. However, the great numbers of individuals looking toward the East, toward Sufi mysticism and Buddhism, for a deeper religious experience betray the heart of a people that has either come alive or feels itself near death. Many Catholics are neither aware of our mystical tradition nor supported in their search for it. Often those who minister in the Church are themselves too busy to attract to our contemplative heritage those who are spiritually thirsty.

The world in which we live is full of images and speed, of technology and hurry, of noise and exhaustion. Everything is a "click" away. Information is at our fingertips. E-mails demand instant responses. We shop from home via cybermalls. Instead of cherishing the extra time we have, we crowd it with more things we feel need to be done. Information about more possibilities creates more potential things to do.

The world of images stimulates us and numbs us. We find our thoughts and desires shaped by what we've seen and heard, rather than arising from deep inside. We crave the silence and solitude that would return us to ourselves.

> After all, a mystic is not a special kind of human being, but every human being is a special kind of mystic.
>
> Br. David Steindl-Rast

One woman found her world transformed in the midst of an everyday visit to a well. There she met someone who told her everything she had ever done, yet loved her just the same. She was one of the hated Samaritans; *he* was the Messiah. She had her place, her image, her label, and her guilt. He lifted her desires and changed her dreams.

The story of the Samaritan woman (see Jn 4:7-15) is a perfect introduction to a book on contemplation. In this woman's experience the rhythm of contemplation unfolds: encounter, engagement, commitment, and perseverance.

The woman in the Gospel story introduces her fellow townspeople to this man, saying: "He told me all I ever did." They came and listened to what Jesus had to say: some out of curiosity, others with a secret hope, others just to make sure they weren't missing out on something big. They were won over by the words and love of Jesus. They told the Samaritan woman they no longer needed to rely on her word about the Teacher; they'd met Jesus for themselves. The introduction had led to a brief period of engagement, then to commitment: they believed in the Messiah, and their lives were changed.

Almost everyone has had some sort of transcendent experience. The Lord has met us at the "wells" of our everyday lives. Sometimes we have even listened to him and recognized the commitment loving him will entail. Maybe we have embraced that commitment. What happens, however, when the initial fire dies out, when responsibility smothers the time we could give to this new relationship, or pulsing techno images glaze our eyes, hiding from them the vision of the transcendent? How do we persevere in an original experience, and what is the reward?

In these pages I seek to address what is one of the single

most important questions for the lay Christian today: What are the practices of spiritual living for a person in a postmodern society? When our souls are thirsty for the spiritual, how do we find the time to contemplate, and more importantly, what do we do during that time? Does the ancient mystical tradition of the Church mean anything today in a world so quickly changing?

This book is meant to be a companion for a relationship with the Lord in the arena of one's daily life. For those who want to contemplate, the *desire* is enough. Let God do the rest.

PART I

ENCOUNTER: THE RHYTHM BEGINS

There was a time not long ago when people lived by the rhythms of nature. These seemingly endless, fairly predictable, cosmic rhythms corresponded integrally to their own rhythms of birth and death, of joy and sorrow, of healing and pain.

In our postmodern age, we have become people who respond to the rhythms created by electronic technology. We turn on the Walkman or CD player, listen to a song, and perhaps tap our feet. Unaccustomed to silence, we keep seeking rhythms to carry us along.

The ancient rhythms of nature are often not easily accessible to us. The rhythms of technology reflect electronic rather than eternal horizons. And so, Christians today have a unique challenge: to discover a personal rhythm that is in harmony with the natural and the eternal. Only then can we hope to encounter God.

Chapter One

Cultivate Stillness and Silence

> [God] said, "Go forth, and stand upon the mount before the Lord." And behold, the Lord passed by, and a great and strong wind rent the mountains, and broke in pieces the rocks before the Lord, but the Lord was not in the wind; and after the wind an earthquake, but the Lord was not in the earthquake; and after the earthquake a fire, but the Lord was not in the fire; and after the fire a still small voice. And when Elijah heard it, he wrapped his face in his mantle and went out and stood at the entrance of the cave.
>
> 1 KINGS 19:11-13

Have you tried to converse with someone in a room full of distractions? A video is playing; another member of the family is practicing a musical instrument; the drone of the lawn mower is eating up the silence. The excessive stimulation makes meaningful conversation impossible.

Some never experience the peace of contemplation because they try to pray in just this type of situation. Perhaps not literally—most people realize that it is difficult to hear God's whisper over a blaring TV. Our noise is on the inside. Our minds grind in an endless conversation—commenting, regretting, expecting, worrying, resenting. Because of these distractions, our encounters with God remain shallow and tentative. Some of the early Desert Fathers called this the ceaseless "murmuring" of our minds. An early abba likened the mind to a tree full of chattering monkeys.

Through a rhythm of quieting and "stilling," of systematic preparation for prayer, we can attune ourselves to the mystery within us. Contemplation begins with the quieting of one's whole lifestyle and being. The following exercise will help you to cultivate this habit of inner stillness.

❧

1. *Prepare yourself.* Sit, kneel, or lie for awhile in a quiet, comfortable place. Perhaps you'll choose a chair with a straight back; perhaps you'll take a cup of tea out on the back porch. Be comfortable. Be alone. Slow down.

2. *Be aware.* Notice what is around you. Observe how you are feeling. Systematically focus your attention on each part of your body: shoulders, neck, arms, hands, stomach, feet.... Tell each part to relax.

3. *Breathe.* Take four long breaths. These can help you distance yourself from the speed and confusion of the office, of getting kids off to school, or of dealing with traffic.

> [The Lord said to me,] "Offer me each little moment as it passes; this will be enough, because then your whole year will be for me."
>
> G. Bossis, *He and I*

The Gift of Quietness

It may be difficult for you to imagine eking out more than a few moments of silence from your busy day. However, there is a large movement—even in the secular business arena—toward silence, religious study, and contemplative experience. The marvel of modern technology is taking its toll on both our emotional capacity for relating and our mental ability to keep pace. The human spirit hungers for the kind of peace found along the ancient way of contemplation.

It may take some creativity and life rearranging, but you *can* find this serenity! Some people rise just a bit earlier in the morning to stake their claim of peace while the world is still asleep. One elderly woman I know has a "prayer chair" in her living room where she spends early morning moments with God. Her rosary hangs on the worn armrest, and her Bible is nearby in an old magazine rack.

If taking advantage of the morning quiet is not an option, find another time that will work for you. Take a daily walk with the Lord. Steal away for a few moments at lunchtime or during morning coffee break to pray. Try lingering a few moments in the evening, after the rest of the house has hushed.

> If you pray with words, let them be filled with love and come from the deepest part of your heart. Pray with great respect and trust. Fold your hands, close your eyes, and lift up your heart to the Lord.... Pray simply. Let your heart speak. Praise the Lord with all your soul.
>
> Mother Teresa

> Let there be a place somewhere in which you can breathe naturally, quietly, and not have to take your breaths in continuous short gasps. A place where your mind can be idle, and forget its concerns, descend into silence, and worship the Father in secret.
>
> Thomas Merton

Giving ourselves these silent moments is crucial to the well-being of our souls. These moments free us from the myth of self-actualization. They also daily remind us of our utter dependence on Christ.

These times of resting restore in us the rhythm God built into our universe from the beginning. Leisure teaches us, as Charles Dickens once said, to have the "keen vision of all that is ordinary," for then "we would hear the grass grow and the roar that is silence." As our spirits cry out to God in our moments of leisure, ours is the promise of peace-filled living, even amidst dirty diapers and teenage tempers.

> It is such rest to know
> that while my boat is tossed on billows' foam—
> now high, now low—
> that raging seas can never overwhelm,
> because my Father's hand is on the helm
> to pilot me safely home.
>
> —Anonymous

Beginning Today ...

1. *Schedule time to relax.* Make a weekly appointment in your calendar for a true leisure break. During this time, plan at least one thing that you really like to do, something that relaxes you.

2. *Take some time to just do nothing.* Doing nothing is the art of letting life reveal itself to you rather than scheduling life's events.

3. *Live in the present.* Take several deep breaths and, forgetting about the future and the past, look around you. Where is there beauty? Where is there need? Let the gift of each moment surprise you with the little pleasures it brings.

> For a little while give your time to God,
> and rest in him for a little.
> Enter the inner chamber of your mind,
> shut out all things save God,
> and having barred the door of your chamber, say to him,
> "Thy face, O Lord, will I seek."
>
> St. Anselm of Canterbury

The Gift of Awareness

Silent moments throughout the day can be links in a chain of prayer. For some, travel time provides moments of silence, time for communion with God. Standing in line is another precious space for silence. Waiting rooms in doctors' offices can also be places where we still our hearts and rest gently in the hands of the Heavenly Father.

Many people use the time before going to sleep to read—a silent activity that engages the emotions and the imagination. Reading the Gospels, the lives of the saints, or a good spiritual book right before falling asleep helps enhance the quiet in our lives.

Each of these moments of silent awareness that we lift up in quiet conversation with God gives us a fresh start. We seek to give our full attention to each moment, not only to these silent moments but to each task, to each person we encounter. Awareness creates interior silence.

It isn't often that we are fully present in the moment in which we are living; usually we are in the past or in the future. It is amazing what happens when we gently but firmly remove everything from our minds except the *now.* Then we begin to notice what is around us and within us. We can care more, think more, and live more.

> This is all he asks of you: that you live and respond to his grace in the here and now.
>
> St. Francis de Sales

❧

Chapter Two

Live Gently on the Earth

Moments of quiet and stillness will be only isolated interludes in our day unless they are part of a rhythm that leads to a gentler lifestyle. Our culture of violence affects us, whether the violence is against those we know and love, against strangers who appear as flickering images on the TV, or even against our environment.

Our actions and decisions are profoundly influenced by the values of our society. We are tempted to overlook the needs of others. We lose the rhythm and the song of centered living. Is it any wonder, then, that between our spaces of contemplation we find ourselves yearning for the music that will carry us from prayer to prayer?

> Long to see God, fear losing God, and find joy in whatever leads to God. Do this, and you'll find great peace.
>
> St. Teresa of Avila

Sister Domenica

Thankfully, there are shining examples of those who embody a gentler way of living. There are still people on the streets of New Jersey and Brooklyn who ask about Sr. Domenica Dolcini, though she has been dead for over forty years. When her grave was opened in 1999, no one was surprised that her body was incorrupt, as beautiful as on the day she was buried.

Born on the outskirts of Rome, Sr. Domenica entered the Daughters of St. Paul at an early age. She was sent to the United States after her profession. On her visits to the people of New York, her smiling "God bless you" became the hallmark of her life. People expectantly waited for her to return with books that nourished their faith and lifted their spirits, hoping to share with her a story, a problem, or a blessing received. The sisters who lived with her still say, "You know, I never once heard Sr. Domenica complain."

After a full day of visiting many people, bringing them the Bible and other religious books, Sr. Domenica worked in the laundry in the evenings. She always took the hardest part of the load. Even though the work was heavy, she opted to make the time light and cheerful. One sister who used to help her remembered how lively those evenings in the laundry were. Sr. Domenica was fun to be with, especially when she played one of her many practical jokes.

Sr. Domenica wasn't known for any type of ecstatic prayer. She would often pray the rosary when she had finished her work. When she prayed in the chapel, she lost track of time. She spent the hours before the Blessed Sacrament in a prayer that was uncomplicated and absorbing. She was only thirty-seven years old when she died, but she is remembered to this day for the twinkle in her eye and the gentleness of her spirit.

Contemplation both emerges out of gentleness and creates gentleness. Gentleness is fostered by little things; you will find a list of some of them in the "Beginning Today" section at the end of this chapter. These seemingly unimportant acts of gentleness train our hearts and minds to open up and receive God's gift of himself in contemplation.

The Gift of Spiritual Intimacy

Although there are a variety of techniques that are intended to help focus one's attention, these are *not* a substitute for prayerful reflection. In fact, we risk doing "violence" to ourselves by applying mind-control techniques that are not intended to draw us closer to the Lord.

It is important to cultivate the freedom to express to the Lord our deepest fears and most hidden secrets. Sputtering thoughts and angry feelings are the ways our spirits call for gentle attention. By offering these distracting thoughts and feelings back to God, we enter into a new level of intimate relationship with him. The following prayer exercise can help empty us of the stress and violence of the world and draw us deeper into the presence of the Lord.

1. *Choose a thirty-minute space for prayer.* Go to that time with nothing special planned.

2. *Begin your prayer by creating atmosphere around you.* Light a candle or burn some incense. Dim the lights or turn them off completely. Place your favorite icon near you—or a statue, painting, flower, or crucifix. Turn on some soft, inspiring music if you'd like.

3. *Sit back and begin to talk to the Father or Jesus or the Holy Spirit.* Share your feelings about what is happening in your life. Reflect upon cherished relationships or troubled ones. Examine your heart and see if there is a recurring feeling that has been dominant for the past day or so.

4. *During this time of prayer, tune in to what is on your mind.* There is one level of "you" that is in gear—the level that is reflecting and addressing God as you pray. Another level of your mind, however, may also be in motion. Many times it takes a little longer to be aware of what this level of your mind is doing.

Listen to the Conversations in Your Mind

Are you aware of any conversations running inside your mind, either with yourself or with someone else? Are you role-playing a situation in which someone has unfairly accused you or hurt you in some way? Or have you been rehearsing all the reasons you feel like a total failure and the cause of every bad thing that has happened?

These conversations create an upset heart. This heart has not been gently held and loved and allowed to reveal what it really feels. The effort to hold this back from one's consciousness results in inner violence.

Discovering the heart's truth brings the whole person into the light and yields inner silence and peace. Listen for the conversations inside: Are you angry with someone? Frustrated? Afraid? Excited? Jealous? Depressed? Angry with yourself? Prejudiced?

Speak to God directly about what you are feeling or are afraid you might feel if you let yourself be fully aware. God speaks to us through what we are feeling. Do not force yourself to feel anything. Simply open yourself.

It may take many thirty-minute prayer periods for you to be able to fully hear what your heart is saying. That is OK. The important thing is to be gentle with your heart's word. Your heart will speak fully when the Spirit knows you are ready. Little by little you will be more attuned to the "sub-text" of your prayer. You will know when your heart is quiet and at peace. You will be alert to when your heart is upset and your mind is in turmoil, and you will then allow that into your prayer so that your whole being is given over to God.

> Set off on the path of prayer with confidence, then swiftly and speedily will you reach the place of peace.
>
> Evagruis

Beginning Today ...

1. *Be thankful for each moment.* Take each moment—good or bad, expected or unexpected, wonderful or painful—as it comes. Try to observe what happens around you without immediately reacting and without judging.

2. *Cultivate habits of gentle living.* Close doors quietly. When driving, keep within the speed limit. Travel back roads sometimes just to enjoy the scenery. Try leaving the radio off when you get into the car.

3. *Practice gentleness toward those around you.* "Do none harm," as St. Thomas More said. Be compassionate to the needs and difficulties of others. Practice forgiveness, and pray for reconciliation.

4. *Cultivate healthy living.* Maintain a healthy diet and exercise routine. Rise early enough each morning so that your day is not rushed.

5. *Find beauty in your world.* Appreciate the beauty of nature all around you. Grow a plant or even a garden. Bring fresh flowers or favorite pictures to work. Visit beautiful places such as art galleries.

6. *Breathe.* Take deep, slow breaths whenever you feel an "anxiety attack" coming on. Remember to leave room in your day just to "be."

~

Chapter Three

Invite God to Come Near

Even as a little girl, I had a relationship with God. I was brought up in a religious atmosphere that seeped into my heart and soul. My mother surrounded us with images and practices that reinforced what we learned about God in school and at the liturgy. My father worshiped beside us, sharing the importance of the spiritual and the transcendent—that world that went beyond what we saw.

One night I felt very strongly the love of God for each person on earth, as well as his sorrow that his love was not wanted by so many whom he had created and loved into life. In a solution only a child would dream up, I told God with all my heart, "You don't have to be sad because some people do not want the love you have to give. I will take it. Give it to me. I will hold on to it until they want it. Then you can have it back to give to them." For me it was a serious moment, this commitment I made. I was waking up to so many things in myself, in others, and in God himself.

This awakening of spirit comes for all of us. God uses surprisingly varied and sometimes casual, everyday events to awaken us to the possibilities of a relationship with him. Annoying circumstances or painful ones can converge into a moment of decision. If we can even faintly feel a nudge in our spirit to openness, we can set out on an adventure of lifelong loving. The call with which God awakens each of us is as unique as our own DNA.

A sudden inspiration or a strong impulse to spontaneously turn to God is not only a call; it is God's revelation of himself to us. At this juncture we have a real choice to make, a choice so profound that all other decisions in our life will hinge on it. Our simple, living "yes" to God is our consent to a gradually more complete revelation of God's sometimes startling but always sublimely loving presence.

> The only One who can teach me to find God is God himself, alone.
>
> Thomas Merton

The Gift of God Himself

Who is this God whom we are choosing? We make the biggest step toward understanding who God is when we begin to reflect on God's self-revelation to each of us.

My spiritual director once asked me how God had revealed himself to me. At that moment, I didn't think God had. As I thought about it, however, I recalled a time in a hospital room when I was recuperating from a stroke. I experienced a strong sensation that someone else was in the room with me, standing at my bedside, watching and waiting. I felt protected and safe. I knew that God was loving me and that I wasn't alone.

Such experiences are God's self-revelation to us. As we compare them with how God has revealed himself in Scripture, slowly we come to know God as he is.

> And how sad if you should suddenly discover that you are full of illusions instead of filled with truth.
>
> M. Wiederkehr

Until we become saturated in this revelation, many of us devise our own image of God. We may endow him with certain characteristics and expectations. We may relate to him as though he were a policeman, a taskmaster, an angry parent, an uninterested spectator of our lives. We may think of him as someone who merely puts up with us, who is never really pleased with us, or who is out to "get us," to catch us at wrong-doing. There are almost as many images of God as there are people, images created by fears and memories, images touched by the media, as well as those shaped by revelation.

Often we do not discover who God really is until our own "gods" no longer do the trick. It is often when our lives have reached their greatest level of chaos that God reveals himself as Peace. After we've run away, God reveals himself as Home. When we are the loneliest, God reveals himself as Friend. When we are the weakest, God becomes our Strength.

In moments like these, when we've come to the end of our own imaginations, we face a door. If we leave the door unopened, it becomes a wall. Open it, risk the unknown, and we enter into the silent, inner chamber of our heart, face to face with God. What has brought us to this door is no longer tragedy. We kiss the ground upon which we've walked. It is grace.

In the inner chamber of our heart, perhaps we're face to face with these images of our own subjective making. It is time to discover who God really is—and who we really are.

1. *Find a restful place for reflection and quiet yourself.* After a few moments, read this short passage from the Gospel of Matthew 3:13-17:

   Then Jesus came from Galilee to the Jordan to John, to be baptized by him. John would have prevented him, saying, "I need to be baptized by you, and do you come to me?" But Jesus answered him, "Let it be so now; for thus it is fitting for us to fulfill all righteousness." Then he consented. And when Jesus was baptized, he went up immediately from the water, and behold, the heavens were opened and he saw the Spirit of God descending like a dove, and alighting on him; and lo, a voice from heaven, saying, "This is my beloved Son, with whom I am well pleased."

2. *Picture the scene.* What time of day is it? Is it cloudy, or is the sun out? How many people are waiting in line to be baptized?

   What does John the Baptist do when he recognizes Jesus? What would *you* do if you realized that Jesus was standing in line with you at the grocery store? Or sitting beside you in a church? Would you feel excited, reverent, nervous? How do you think John felt?

   When Jesus came out of the water, the heavens opened and the Father revealed himself by saying, "This is my beloved Son. Listen to him." In the Gospels, whenever Jesus and the Father speak with each other, it is as if they are pouring themselves out for each other. There seems to be no limit to the love expressed in their communication.

3. *Consider: How has God revealed himself to you in your life?* Do not dwell on the way you *think* about God. Look instead for those "caught-by-surprise" moments when you knew something to be so real that you couldn't doubt it. If you have never before thought about how God has revealed himself to you, you may, at first, conclude that God *hasn't* revealed himself. You might think of occasions when you feel you *should have* experienced his revelation. Gently stay with the question, asking the Spirit to help you.

4. *Jot down these experiences in a notebook.* Note the details of each event, how you felt, and what it meant for you. Relive the experience as completely as you can. God's self-revelation to you will also reveal you to yourself. Talk to God about how you feel, the movements in your heart, and any desires that may be aroused.

> Never will the soul reach its final perfection,
> For it will never encounter a limit....
> It will always be transformed into a better thing.
>
> Gregory of Nyssa
>
> In the polyphonic melody of becoming, the soul perceives an echo of the divine infinity to which she aspires, and she risks letting herself be seduced by its very beauty.
>
> Hans Urs von Balthasar

The Gift of Truth

Many influences contribute to our perception of God and his attitude toward us: our family situation when we were growing up, our relationships with parents and teachers, our religious experiences, as well as other factors. Sometimes we can come through all this history feeling worthless, as though we were "damaged goods." We may feel that God is against us or doesn't care what happens to us.

Until we expose these lies about God and about ourselves, until we root them out and replace them with truth, we will know only our illusions of God. We will never really contemplate *him.*

Naming our misbeliefs and confronting them with the truth demands first of all that we compare them with what God has said about himself and ourselves in his Word.

> With everlasting love I will have compassion on you,
> says the Lord, your Redeemer.
> O afflicted one, storm-tossed, and not comforted,
> behold, I will set your stones in antimony,
> and lay your foundations with sapphires.
>
> ISAIAH 54:8,11

> They who wait for the Lord shall renew their strength,
> they shall mount up with wings like eagles,
> they shall run and not be weary,
> they shall walk and not faint.
>
> ISAIAH 40:31

The Lord is good,
a stronghold in the day of trouble;
he knows those who take refuge in him.

NAHUM 1:7

It was you who drew me from the womb
and soothed me on my mother's breast.
On you was I cast from my birth,
from the womb I have belonged to you.

PSALM 22:9-10, NAB

We must reject those images of God that contradict what he has revealed of himself. We need to repeat again and again:

"In everlasting love he has taken pity on me."

"From the womb I have belonged to him."

"God loves me. He has made me good, lovable, and valuable."

Say these words aloud. Write them in your journal. Take the time to contemplate God as he has made himself known to you. Sit with those experiences, soak in them, turn them over and over again in your mind and heart. As Julian of Norwich said, you have to get to the point where you believe that *you* make the Father dance for joy.

> I love you and you love me and our love shall never be broken.
>
> Jesus to Blessed Julian of Norwich

Love makes us free to laugh, to enjoy life, to be grateful, to make mistakes, to risk, to forgive and be forgiven. God does love us. God wants us to be happy. We can trust him so much that we don't have to be afraid of tomorrow. We don't have to hide, not even when we have fallen.

Chapter Four

Prepare to Ascend the Heights

Settling into a more balanced life or a deeper spiritual life brings with it its own effervescence or "high." The effects are noticed immediately. The cluster of everyday decisions are reorganized to make room for new practices and priorities. We can feel as though we have joined a new elite, one with special secrets that raise us above the common grind of daily living. It's possible to think that this is it! The contemplative life is ours!

The danger in this case is to stop: to mistake the doorway for the ballroom, a first encounter with marriage, a tentative meeting with intimate knowledge. The rhythm begun is only a technique to assist us in relaxation and a more ordered life. By itself it cannot yield the fruits of contemplation.

The attempt at entering into this sacred rhythm has turned over the field of our consciousness. We become aware of our souls in new and startling ways. Leisure may be the means God uses to open us up to see our hearts as never before. The rhythm of gentleness sometimes can reveal to us the depths of our anger and inner violence. The rhythm of silence can reveal to us our inner voices, the skeletons in our closets, the past. We can embrace ourselves intimately and at the same time discover aspects of ourselves we do not like.

We may be frightened by what we see, attempt to reject,

hide, or change it. This lowliness was not what we expected. What we want is the heights of contemplation.

> You enter a self-contained world of deliberations, resolutions, and expectations. Suddenly you remember that you are permitted to pray, and for a moment everything else disappears. Prayer streams into you, from all sides, as perfect refreshment for the spirit, without your needing to see or to think anything in particular.
>
> Adrienne von Speyr

The Gift of Exalted Lowliness

The mystical life today goes by some pseudo-names that distort its meaning. We may want "enlightenment." We may want "perfection." We may want "illumination." The contemplative life, mystical prayer, is about none of these things. It is about what *God* wants.

When we come right down to it, we want to be big, important, and successful in our eyes, in God's eyes, and in the eyes of others. However, in the Gospel we read instead a story of chosen weakness, glorified poverty, exalted lowliness. God will never take away our poverty, for then he would take away exactly what we need to depend on him. He wants us to realize that we can't achieve salvation and grow in contemplation by ourselves. Actually, we will get absolutely nowhere by ourselves.

We think if we are good, if we get an A+ on our spiritual report card, the divine Teacher will like us and we will be assured a seat in the next grade. But the spiritual life doesn't work that way. We can do nothing by ourselves. St. Paul says, "For we are his [God's] workmanship, created in Christ Jesus for good works, which God prepared beforehand, that we should walk in them" (Eph 2:10).

This revelation of our own poverty, our misery that we can't perfect ourselves, is an invitation. It is time to make a giant leap of faith.

To become a contemplative, one must simply start to contemplate. I say *simply* because to begin to contemplate one must be able to honestly begin where one is; just start, and nothing more. No expectations. No achievements. No stories to tell of wisdom gained. One simply must just begin. And after fifty years of contemplating God every day, one must begin the first day of the fifty-first year in the same way. Begin with the simple desire to contemplate, reaching out to God, believing that God is sustaining with love the one who longs to see his face.

Christian mysticism is *God's* work. Gradually we must abandon our striving. We must abandon even our desire for perfection. We learn not to trust anything to ourselves because we cannot know where we are on this strange but beautiful *mystical* path. We may think we know where we've been, but often we seem to have returned to where we were and to be beginning all over again.

Contemplation can only be lived when we turn ourselves over to the adventure and lose ourselves in loving. We need to forget ourselves and our imperfections and reach out in loving trust. God can make us holy in an instant. But usually he takes us through the long and winding path of engagement, commitment, and perseverance. Our part is faith.

~

PART II

ENGAGEMENT: THE PRACTICE OF PRAYER

Engagement is a time of desires and dreams. Two people, two futures, two desires, give way to a common vision and a common hope. An engaged couple spends much time together, discovering preferences and letting down their guard to one another, little by little. As they share more of themselves with each other, they become comfortable in each other's presence and experience a growing feeling of joy together.

Through the rhythm of stillness, gentleness, and silence we have begun to put into place spaces, attitudes, and actions that are conducive to a serious relationship with God. That relationship is developed more completely through the mystical life—a fancy term for the simple act of prayer. Our hearts long to soar beyond the boundaries of this world and our own human limitations. But to soar beyond we must delve within. God is there, offering himself to be known and loved by us.

The daily space of contemplation, the time we consistently set aside to pray, is about divine engagement. Of course, an engagement with God is vastly different from the human variety. Divine engagement is not a meeting between two equal parties. We do not go to God. The three Persons of the Trinity—Father, Son, and Spirit—draw us toward themselves and place in us a love, a "yes" to their presence and work within us, and a peaceful fullness. This comes from them, but at the same time it points to a core within ourselves, a transcendent calling, God's own desiring that makes us *be.*

> God dwells within you. You are yourself the tabernacle, his secret hiding place. Rejoice, exult, for all you could possibly desire, all your heart's longing is so close, so intimate as to be within you; you cannot *be* without him.
>
> St. John of the Cross

Our desires and God's desires meet again and again in the fire of encounter. As we learn God's desires for us, as he reveals himself more deeply, we realize the tinseled glitter of many of our own desires and needs. Gradually we come to desire the desires of God himself, letting God desire in us. Jean-Claude Sagne says, "The Spirit makes our desire live from the life of God himself, to the point where God himself comes to desire at the heart of our desire."

As a marital engagement takes time, so these next seven chapters are meant to take time. They are not *about* prayer; they *are* prayer. Each prayer exercise is a "date" with the beloved One.

To Help You Get Started

1. *Make your time with God a priority.* You may want to choose a certain time each day to pray, and schedule your life and work around that sacred time.

2. *Don't try to "get it right."* You will find variations on all these forms of prayer, depending upon which books you read. You may even develop your own unique style, incorporating more than one prayer form. The

important part of your experience is not the method but the encounter with God.

3. *Repeat each exercise.* Work through the exercise where it is indicated in the chapter, then again at the end. Or you may want to make a weekly mini-retreat, spending time with one chapter each week.

4. *Record your impressions.* Keep a journal. After each prayer time, make a couple of notes regarding how it went, what you were feeling, and any difficulties you encountered.

5. *Take it a step further.* If one of the prayer exercises is particularly helpful, check your local Christian bookstore or library for other books on the subject. Or if you would like to talk with someone knowledgeable, ask for recommendations for potential spiritual directors from your parish, your diocesan office for spiritual development, or a local convent or Catholic college. Or perhaps there is a prayer group that meets in your area for specific types of prayer—centering prayer, *lectio divina,* or Ignatian contemplation.

6. *Most importantly, give yourself time.* While you are working through this section, you might also want to be reading the next two sections on commitment and perseverance. Though a relationship can be dissected into stages for discussion of its development, in reality you are in all stages at all times. Feel free to flip back and forth among the chapters and read what the Spirit inspires you to read.

Though you may be reading different parts of this book at the same time, remember to keep a steady and consistent pace. Try these prayer styles on for size, discerning where you are more attracted and what you find most helpful. Remember that the way you pray may change throughout your life—and sometimes even throughout your day.

Chapter Five

Remain in God's Presence: Lessons From the Life of Brother Lawrence

Stroll the aisle of your local department store where calendars and appointment books are displayed—especially in the first weeks of January! Everyone is urgently trying to keep control of his or her life. Often our time has been scrupulously planned days beforehand. Sometimes we have packed so much into one day, it seems that not one more thing could be squeezed into it. Then we remember an appointment we'd forgotten.

All too often, it is the intangible and spiritual aspect of life that is set aside for "later." How do we fit one more practice into a day that is already overrun with things to do?

> Nothing could be of more value in our crowded lives than to take five minutes from our day to stop, breathe deeply and think of God.
>
> Ettie Hillesum
> Died in Auschwitz

About Br. Lawrence

Br. Lawrence of the Resurrection (born Nicolas Herman) was a sixteenth-century Carmelite monk. Poorly educated, this French monk spent thirty years toiling in the monastery kitchen. He has left us a legacy on the highest contemplation for those who cannot avail themselves of the luxury of a lengthy time of prayer. His classic work is called *The Practice of the Presence of God.* It has not been out of print since its first appearance in 1692.

Br. Lawrence discovered after he entered the monastery that he could not meditate for long periods of time. The time instead was spent in trying to get rid of stray thoughts. He thought about what he had done during the day, what he needed to do, what he wanted to do, what he had forgotten to do. When he had finished "praying," Br. Lawrence could not even say what he had been praying about!

Br. Lawrence resolved his problem by turning his entire day into a conversation with God. He praised and thanked God, talked to him about what needed to be done, asked his help, and offered him his work. And if he forgot God, and the "connection" was dropped for a long period of time, he went back and told God he was sorry and picked up his prayer again.

> My wish is that you give enough free time to God that he can make clear to you what he desires: and especially that he can reach that in you which is most alive. If you do not have "hours" at your disposal, then give your moments, your instants of time.
>
> Madeleine Delbêl

The Love of God Is Everything

The spiritual guidance Br. Lawrence offers is simple: the love of God is everything, a love that surrounds and enfolds us. Out of this love should proceed a rhythm of continual internal awareness of God. Our constant conversation with God helps us to remember that he is our partner in everything we do. Br. Lawrence used to say to the Lord, "So that my work will be better, Lord, work with me; receive my work and possess all my affections."

Just as two people who love each other find their days filled with thoughts of each other, so in this practice we raise our minds to remember the One who loves us most. We establish a loving, familiar union with God, who holds us in the palm of his gentle hand. The practice of the presence of God becomes a habitual state of the soul, an openness to the Divine One who surrounds us in our busy lives. The following exercise will help you to "practice" this divine Presence.

Speaking with God about everything that happens in our day is so simple it can be elusive when we try to practice it daily. In its simplicity it brings together life and prayer in one unending conversation.

1. *Choose several days* or segments of time on several days to practice the presence of God.

2. *Speak to God about everything* that happens or that doesn't happen, about how you feel and how you wish you were feeling, about things that go right and things that go absolutely wrong.

3. *Try to notice if there is a difference* in the tone of your day, in your attitude, thought patterns, or mood. Perhaps you were surprised by thoughts that had never occurred to you before or new ways of dealing with an old situation. Perhaps you felt that at last you weren't alone and had someone with whom to share every burden. Perhaps you forgot to speak with God more often than you remembered to.

4. *Before retiring at night, speak with God again* as if he were right beside you. He is.

The Gift of God's Presence

As we become more "taken" with the experience of God's presence, it becomes foolish, even difficult, to leave aside conversation with God and let our minds become filled with trivial things and worries. Worry gets us nowhere, planning gets us somewhere, but conversing with Love gets us everywhere, and our work gets done easily and restfully.

> We shall be blessed with clear vision if we keep our eyes fixed on Christ. As no darkness can be seen by anyone absorbed in light, so no trivialities can capture the attention of anyone who has his eyes on Christ.
>
> St. Gregory of Nyssa

This conversing with God, the rhythm of God's presence as it affects our lives, leads to some other profound revelations.

God loves us and cares for us. When a certain task is difficult or distasteful, conversing with God turns these things into prayer. Somehow God almost does them for us.

When God is our highest priority, everything else falls into place. When the work we need to do, the places we need to go, the appointments we need to keep, begin to take second place to a contemplative stance, our priorities begin to straighten out. Yet the work does not just get *done*, it gets done *better*. We get done what we need to get done, but without stress and hurry. We keep our appointments and they yield more fruitful results.

Our struggle to overcome bad habits and sin becomes much easier, for we need only say to God, "My God, I do not know how to do it, and I can't unless you enable me to do it." God will come to our aid immediately, because it is true: Without God we can do nothing good.

We are free from the compulsion to "fix" ourselves. Relying on the gift of God's own life that he wishes to give us, Br. Lawrence would have us pray: "Lord, if you leave me alone, this is all I am capable of doing. You must prevent me from falling. You must correct in me what is not good. It is all up to you." We learn to behave very simply with God, speaking with him about things as they happen.

Practicing God's presence helps us "tune out" negative and impulsive thoughts. Many unhappy conversations that bring disturbance to ourselves and others begin with our thoughts:

"See what she is doing."

"Did you hear what he said?"

"I can't believe they are doing that!"

"Doesn't anyone care about me?"

There *are* situations that demand study, confrontation, and action. But if we are honest, most situations really do not concern us. If we want peace, thoughts that have nothing to do with our present duties or our salvation should be replaced with a conversation with God, a prayer for the other person, and an inward serenity. Limiting our involvement in other people's affairs when they don't have any impact on us is a healthy way to find more time for contemplation.

Br. Lawrence encourages us to think about God during the day and at night, in our occupations and our leisure, in the car and at work, in our kitchens and in front of the TV or computer. God is always near. We don't want to leave God by himself. He is within our hearts, always visiting us.

For all eternity we will be conversing with God, so Br. Lawrence encourages us to start now. Let's worship him without ceasing. Live with him. Die with him. This is the joy of being a Christian.

> The time of business is no different from the time of prayer. In the noise and clatter of my kitchen, I possess God as tranquilly as if I were upon my knees before the Blessed Sacrament.
>
> Br. Lawrence of the Resurrection

Chapter Six

Let the Spirit Direct You: Lessons From the Life of St. Ignatius of Loyola

> Our only desire and our one choice should be this: I want and I choose what better leads to God's deepening his life in me.
>
> St. Ignatius,
> as paraphrased by David L. Fleming, S.J.

I remember participating in a retreat one time, and feeling ull held back, resistant. I was praying with a crowd scene in the 'Gospel of Mark.

As I was meditating, I imagined myself in the crowd. Suddenly Jesus approached me and took me by the hand. H started to walk with me so fast down the road, just the two of us, could barely keep up. I realized as I saw myself there on e road that I couldn't keep up because I didı want to go with Jesus. I really didn't want to be with him at all. The more I dragged my feet, the faster he walked. As stayed with this feeling of being dragged along, I realized Jesus was actually dragging me past my resistance and my laziness and my dullness.

Finally, I ran out in front of him and held up my hand for him to stop. I didn't say a word. I turned around and set off in a dead run in the direction Jesus had been taking me. He ran ahead of me and I followed him once more, but this time I ran after him with joy. From that moment on my life has never been the same.

Contemplation is ultimately about finding God in all things. Taking time to pray silently heightens our awareness of the Spirit working in us and of the Lord who is telling us something. Through regularly praying with the Scriptures and encountering Jesus in prayer we keep alive the faith-dimension within us. We more clearly and energetically direct our lives toward God and seek him as the deepest Source of our existence, not only with our heads, but also with our hearts.

St. Ignatius' own personal experience, and the directives of prayer that he left as a legacy to all those who pray, rest upon some basic foundations. Some of these foundations are:

- Tracing our experiences back to their source,
- Staying in lasting contact with the Source, and
- Keeping in touch with the innermost part of ourselves as it lives before God's face.

In this prayer of intimacy with the Lord, we overcome estrangement and illusions. It is a prayer that focuses on God's great love for us and on how that great love is made manifest in the experiences of our lives.

About St. Ignatius of Loyola

The life of St. Ignatius of Loyola was intricately bound up with the method of contemplation, spiritual growth, and examination that would become his legacy to us.

Born in 1491 in the Basque section of Spain, young Ignatius

dreamed of winning women, becoming a valiant soldier, conquering the world. However, his military career came to an abrupt end when, at the age of thirty, he was wounded in battle while fighting for the Duke of Nájera in France. Ignatius was sent to his family's castle in Loyola to recuperate.

He had plenty of time for reflection during the long months of recuperation. The seeds of the *Spiritual Exercises of St. Ignatius* and his understanding of consolation and desolation were born in these days. Ignatius' conversion occurred the same year that Martin Luther took up residence in the castle at Wartburg during his own crisis.

After receiving a vision of the Blessed Virgin, Ignatius made a pilgrimage to Montserrat to venerate Mary at a famous shrine there. He then settled in Manresa, where in 1522 he made a rough draft of his *Spiritual Exercises.* On the feast of the Assumption in 1534, Ignatius and six companions, including St. Francis Xavier, gathered in a chapel in Montmartre and vowed to live in poverty and chastity and to go to Palestine to preach the Gospel. However, their plans were impeded by hostilities between Venice and the Turks. The group went to Rome, where Ignatius was ordained a priest in 1538 and the Society of Jesus was approved two years later.

During his convalescence and through the years that led up to his founding the Society of Jesus, Ignatius had learned that our own experiences play an important role in positively directing us to God. By paying close attention to our experiences and our feelings, we can discover how God reveals himself in the movements of our hearts and minds. Through a contemplation that involves our whole being, we directly communicate with the Lord who also reveals himself to us.

Once, I was meditating on Jesus calling the disciples. I went up to him and told him that I wanted to come with him too. Jesus turned around and walked away from me without a word. It took me awhile to realize the alienation I felt from Jesus, and how the Spirit working in my heart was making me aware of this. Several years of prayer and healing passed before I realized that Jesus no longer walked away from me when I put myself in the apostles' shoes, but rather stopped me even before I asked him anything by holding me in his arms. My experience, my feelings about myself, and my prayer came together in a contemplation that helped me find God in my life in new ways.

> Union with God is a song that does not die in the hearing, a flavor which does not abate in the eating, an embrace which gives delight without end.
>
> St. Augustine

Ignatius would have us contemplate Christ in the Gospels by placing ourselves somewhere in the scene, participating in the conversation and activity, and allowing God the liberty of revealing himself to us.

1. *Prepare yourself for prayer.* Quiet your mind. Ask God to reveal himself. Tell him what you desire of him in this time of prayer.

2. *Talk to Jesus.* Ask him to speak to you through the Scripture you are about to read.

3. *Choose a story from the Gospel.* For example, let's choose the story of the storm on the lake (see Mk 7:42-45). Read the passage slowly several times, leaving a few moments of silence between readings.

4. *Imagine yourself in that Gospel scene.* Smell the air, feel the water as it pounds the boat and splashes you in the face, run your hand along the edge of the vessel so precariously thrown about in the storm. Talk to the other men there. See Jesus asleep.

5. *Let your feelings surface.* Is there someone in the story you identify with? Someone you feel repulsed by? Something that makes you afraid or joyful, that attracts or distracts you? Stay with the feelings and central core that seem to be grabbing at your imagination. Forget the rest of the story for now.

   Let things happen in the scene that aren't described in the Gospels. Let's say you feel angry that Jesus doesn't wake up right away. Maybe you're so angry you go back and shake him by the shoulders and tell him to his face exactly how you feel. You can't believe the compassion and love in Jesus' eyes as he listens.

   Or perhaps it doesn't even occur to you to wake Jesus up. You try to solve the problem on your own. As you are trying to stabilize the vessel, Jesus comes to you and asks you a simple question. What is that question? That question will have something to do with your life experiences, your desires of God, your feelings about yourself. What is it like for you to have the storm calmed?

6. *Remain in the scene for as long as it is nourishing your prayer.* You may choose to continue your prayer until you feel a shift. Or maybe you need to repeat the meditation over several days or weeks until you come to a moment of peace and faith.

7. *End your prayer time with a period of silence and the Our Father.* You may find it useful to record your impressions in a spiritual journal.

The Gifts of Consolation and Desolation

In our hectic, image-filled, and noisy lives, it is not always easy to get in touch with our deepest feelings due to the over-abundance of impressions all around us. We rarely know what we most desire—deep-down desires. Sometimes we haven't the courage to ask. Many times, prayer consists in speaking about God or about ourselves to God, rather than speaking directly to God and letting him deal directly with us.

As we imagine ourselves in the scenes of the Gospel, we learn about God and about ourselves from our reactions, our attractions, our resistances. Ignatius began to see two distinct movements. When he read the Gospel and imagined himself imitating the saints, he felt a peace that lasted. He felt drawn to God, and he felt a growth in faith, hope, and charity. When, instead, he imagined himself courting beautiful ladies, the joy that he experienced ended quickly, only to be replaced with dullness. He named these two movements (or responses) *consolation* and *desolation.*

As we become more prayerful people, we can learn to discern, among the inner movements of our minds and hearts, those that arise under the prompting of the Holy Spirit or the prompting of something contrary to the Holy Spirit.

Discernment

When we experience a movement out toward others and toward God, when we feel a deep peace along with a growth in faith (even if it may be during a situation of personal pain or suffering), the Spirit is influencing our lives. Jarring feelings, dullness, and alienation from God often accompany a movement away from God.

Ignatius was attentive to his feelings and experiences in prayer and throughout the day. Listening to our feelings is an exercise in authenticity—of bringing our whole self to God in prayer so that he can reveal himself to us and what he desires of us. The following is an exercise in attentiveness and openness to God working within.

Place yourself in the presence of the Lord and pray for enlightenment. Relax. Breathe deeply. Run quickly over the day, allowing your real feelings to surface, the ones you've buried so that you could make it through the day.

Pay attention to the way in which the Lord has been present to you. For instance, did you feel drawn to the Lord anytime during the day through a book, or music, or a segment of a show you were watching? Did you meet the Lord when you felt afraid, misunderstood, tempted, happy, relieved? Did the presence of God come alive in new ways during the liturgy or when you were reading Scripture or at prayer?

How has the Lord moved you today? Have you moved from confidence in yourself to dependence on him? From your plans at any cost to his plans whatever the cost? From self-hatred to greater acceptance of yourself? Have you felt moved to go out of yourself and reach into the lives of others, friends and enemies alike?

Has something happened for which you should be especially grateful? How are you looking toward the future? With anticipation or with fear? Is there some area in your life in which the Lord is calling you to conversion?

Choose one incident or reaction that stands out particularly for you at this time. Ask yourself if you are in consolation:

- Is the experience moving you toward God?
- Are you more accepting of others?
- Have you become more sensitive and gentle?
- Do you have a more realistic view of yourself?
- If the incident is painful, are you sad because God has been offended?
- Underneath tension or conflict, is there a sense of faith?
- Are you turned out of yourself and toward others?

Or ask yourself if you are in desolation:

- Do you feel more turned in on yourself?
- Has God slipped out of your consciousness?
- Is he no longer a part of your activities?
- Do you feel alone and separated from God, even though you desire to be with him?
- Does everything seem confused or difficult?
- Are you "happy," but with a sense that you are fooling yourself?

- Is the experience moving you away from the Lord?
- Are you keeping things in perspective?

Knowing God's Presence

Spend some time talking over these things with the Lord. If you are in consolation and are moving toward the Lord, thank him for his goodness and his love. If you are in desolation, turn to God with confidence. Try to determine if this movement away from the Lord is because you have forgotten him or offended him. On the other hand, this experience of searching for God without any feeling of success may be God's way of teaching you that his presence and your prayer are gifts, not the reward of your efforts.

Desolation and consolation follow each other in waves. When you are feeling consoled and close to God you should gain strength, so that during those times when you feel far from him you will remember and wait for the desolation to pass. If you are in desolation, Ignatius suggests that you re-double your efforts in prayer and meditation, make some sacrifice, and talk over the situation with a good spiritual director.

For five centuries the teachings of Ignatius have pointed the way for Christians yearning for spiritual transformation. The means he gave us include the contemplation of the Gospels, the examination of conscience, the *Spiritual Exercises,* and discernment of spirits. What unites all these practices, what makes them truly Ignatian, is the recommendation to observe our hearts carefully in order to find out which feelings make it easier for us to believe, hope, and love, and which lead to want of faith, hope, and love.

Ignatius echoes the words of St. Paul in his Letter to the Galatians: Do my experiences and feelings make the fruits of the Spirit—love, joy, peace, patience, kindness, goodness, faithfulness, gentleness, and self-control—grow or diminish (see Gal. 5:22)? This is the compass by which Ignatius kept course in his life. The movements within him became the yardstick by which he measured all his choices. Ignatius' deepest desire was to seek and to do God's will. In this quest, the feelings of his own God-centered heart were decisive.

In contemplation, to live in daily imitation of Jesus, to serve as an apostle in whatever way God desires, becomes the very energy of our lives. As the experience continues, our hearts are stretched beyond what we ever thought possible: we are so transformed, so identified with Jesus, that we become, we are Jesus in and for the world.

> Lord, help me be a soul of prayer; help me that all my works swim in prayer.
>
> Blessed Pauline von Mallinckrodt

~

Chapter Seven

Experiencing the Longing to Touch God: Lessons From *Lectio Divina*

After we have prayed awhile, we discover a longing for a deeper and deeper prayer—something beyond a monologue or even a conversation with God, beyond intercessions, complaints, or the expression of our feelings in honest dialogue. We long to touch God. We open ourselves to a personal knowledge of him who is Love itself.

The more we approach God, the more he reveals himself to us. Paradoxically, God's revelation of himself to us is detected by our senses in such things as darkness, aridity, and worst of all, a trembling realization of our own inadequacies. When Light approaches, he exposes our darkness.

At this point we may find *lectio divina*, the prayerful reading of God's Word, our teacher, our discipline, and our revealer. Maybe the Word causes us to notice our temper for the first time, or perhaps our selfishness, or an uncharitable attitude. Maybe we see a prejudice, ambition, or practice that blocks further growth into Love. The call of Triune Love brings to light in us whatever hinders a full and complete response to that call.

As we sit with the Word—reading, meditating, praying, contemplating—we feel the need to reconcile ourselves with the One who is *the* Word. The pain we experience is like that caused by a surgeon who is healing a wound. The way to peace is self-surrender into the hands of a merciful Father, who knows our weaknesses and loves us through them.

> Holy Spirit, Goodness, Supreme Beauty!
> O you whom I adore, O you whom I love!
> Consume with your divine flames
> This body and this heart and this soul!
> This spouse of the Trinity
> Who desires only your will!
>
> Blessed Elizabeth of the Trinity

About *Lectio Divina*

Lectio divina, one of the most time-tested methods of deeper prayer, has come down to us from very early in the Church, the era of the great monastic movements. It is a path of sacred reading, of resting in the Word and letting oneself be shaped and held by it. These movements—from reading to meditation to prayer to contemplation—form the disciple in his or her union with God. As we say "yes" to the Spirit, without holding back, and recognize our littleness before the infinite power of God, he can raise us up to heights beyond our imaginings. Let him do the work. Ours is simply to trust.

Lectio divina consists of four steps. The first is *reading (lectio)* and listening. The power of the Holy Spirit operates actively in each phrase of what we read, especially if we are reading Sacred Scripture. The grace of the Holy Spirit penetrates our minds and hearts when we welcome the Word with love and open attention.

The next step is *meditation (meditatio),* a step of deepening.

We reread several times a passage of Scripture. As the Word moves from the head to the heart, we become inflamed with the Word and embrace the Love that is speaking to us.

Meditation moves us naturally to the third step, *prayer (oratio)*, the heart-to-heart opening to God. We become available to the intimate work of the Holy Spirit in our souls. We move naturally between meditation and prayer as we experience God at the core of our being.

In this realm of illumination we become acutely aware of who God is and who we are. Here our shortcomings and lack of love become painfully apparent. We see the vast difference between where we are and our ultimate goal—union with God. Yet we still feel drawn, and Love leads us on to the fourth step, union or *contemplation (contemplatio)*.

❧

Ideally, the text for one's *lectio* should be chosen before one begins to pray—even the night before. It can be read over once so that the seed of the Word has a chance to fall to the "earth" and begin to germinate even while you sleep.

What should one read in *lectio divina*? The Scriptures are preferred. The Fathers of the church and writings of the saints are other possibilities. Whatever you choose should be "solid food," in the words of St. Paul, steeped and time-tested in tradition.

1. *Focus.* When the time for prayer has arrived, find a quiet place where you will not be interrupted. Take time to focus your attention. Your posture should be alert but not tense, helping you remain attentive.

2. *Take up the text and begin to read slowly.* In the past, monks read the passage aloud in a soft voice, so that not only the mind participated in the reading but the ears and the voice as well. Even today it is a good idea to read a passage over slowly and softly several times, pausing between each reading. As you pause, do not try to reflect on the meaning of the text. Continue simply to keep your mind at rest. Let the Word fall on its own under the weight of grace, and wait for the surprise of its revelation.

3. *Pay attention to what you feel.* While reading, you may find that a certain word or phrase jumps out at you, ablaze with sudden meaning. If you are especially distracted because of other concerns, you may find that you need to read the passage more times than usual, each time reading fewer and fewer verses, slowly honing in on the particular gift the passage reveals to you. If you feel "dry" or unaffected by what you read, you may find that you barely get beyond this point, jumping into prayer and then a wordless pleading.

4. *Move to meditation,* prayerfully pondering and reflecting upon the word or phrase that has sparked your interest. Something there is waiting to reveal itself. That something is in direct relation to your life: something you desire, a need you have, a problem you are experiencing, or some aspect of your personality that needs redemption.

5. *Gently turn your heart toward God in prayer.* Later you may find it helpful to record your thoughts in your prayer journal while the experience is still fresh in your mind.

"Come to Me"—Meditation

Perhaps an example would help to guide you initially. In Luke 10:38-41 we find that "Mary ... sat down at the Lord's feet and listened to him speaking." The words "sat down at the Lord's feet" might take on a living meaning. Sitting down at the Lord's feet requires one to find the Lord, to know the Lord, to trust the Lord as a friend. This leads us to consider any number of questions:

- Am I attracted to those words because I feel alone and without friends?
- Do I consider Jesus a friend?
- Have I distanced myself from God? If so, why? Who is God for me? Am I afraid of him? Why?
- Do I really know God? If not, why not? Have I squeezed my relationship with God out of my things-to-do list?

It is important to allow ourselves to be fully present in this experience. What is our current reality? How would we like it to be?

We might recall other verses from the Gospel where Jesus beckons people to come to him. "Come to me, all who labor and are heavy laden, and I will give you rest" (Mt 11:28). Picture Jesus washing the feet of his friends at the Last Supper. Stay with the meditation in silence, until prayer spontaneously arises: a prayer of adoration and awe, of sorrow or desire.

Encountering God in His Word—Prayer

Meditation is essential to the forming of Christian life. The goal of prayer is not thoughts about God, however, but a living, breathing encounter with God. This genuine encounter takes place in contemplation, and *oratio* (prayer) prepares us for it. That is why we cannot stop with meditation, for in doing so we have short-circuited the process.

Prayer is a movement out of ourselves and a thrust toward God. Or, conversely, it can be a thrust toward our deepest center, where God makes his home in us. The reflections of the meditation naturally fall into the rhythm of intercessions of a heart that has become newly aware. Modeled on liturgical prayer, our prayer should address the Father—offering him praise and thanksgiving, expressing to him what has deeply moved us and how we experience our need for him—and end by offering the prayer through Christ and in the Holy Spirit. It need not be long. Its formality will decrease as you pray daily for a period of time. A sign of growth in prayer is this simplification and a familiarity with God. This moment of prayer is the hinge leading to *contemplatio* (contemplation).

Heart Speaks to Heart—Contemplation

Thelma Hall, R.C., who has been engaged in ongoing spiritual direction since 1974, reflects in her book, *Too Deep for Words,* that in contemplation, "we now not only love God but are beginning to 'fall *in* love'; i.e., he is becoming the realized center of our lives, and we begin to experience the longing of lovers for union: the desire to be totally given, and totally received."

Contemplation (*contemplatio*) is the school of waiting—the stage where we relinquish our resistance and are mellowed by silence. This final stage of *lectio divina* is framed in stillness and deep recollection. We are at home, and we wait to be visited by God. "God often pays us a visit," says Tauler, a fourteenth-century Dominican preacher and mystic, "but most of the time we are not at home." In the words of Salvail, "In '*contemplatio*' we are doing an apprenticeship in a long and patient shedding which will lead us toward faithfulness."

Contemplation is not something we achieve on our own. Neither is it something we can learn. It is the ripe fruit of reading the Word, in which the Word himself encounters us, overwhelms us, and transforms us. For our part, we sink into silence and patient waiting, we allow the fruit to grow within, we sit and do nothing ourselves because God has taken over and is doing everything. We feel nothing. We have no guarantee but the faithfulness of God. And in that faithfulness, we express our trust by spending a period of time in silent prayer, in contemplation. Little by little, as daily we do our sacred reading, this time of silence will take on a beautiful fascination.

> What matters in the contemplative life is ... to be heroically faithful to grace and to love. If God calls you to him, then he implicitly promises you all the graces you need to reach him. You must be blindly faithful to this promise.
>
> Thomas Merton

Lectio divina opens us to a more intimate resting in God. This form of contemplation is fruitful not only for the mystic in the monastery but also for the mystic in the professional world, or on the bus, or on the soccer field watching her son make his first goal. Loving communion with God is a vital part of everyday life. It is more necessary for the soul than breathing is for the body.

The Spirit Comes

Primary in *lectio divina,* or any other form of contemplative prayer, is the work of the Holy Spirit. In the Holy Spirit we connect deeply to the life of the Trinity. Jesus promised the Holy Spirit to his apostles and to those who would follow him, "believing without seeing." We see the Spirit's power at Pentecost when in prayer the apostles and Mary are flooded with his presence and pushed to the earth's farthest bounds to preach and teach in courageous ways.

It is the Spirit who opens our hearts when we pray. He draws us to a life of union with the Trinity. Jesus' gift of the Spirit is our union with him in the Spirit for the glory of the Father! As children with Jesus the Divine Child, we too can address the Father as "Abba," a term of endearment and total trust. Our immersion in the Trinity becomes the life and nourishment of our souls in an eternity begun today, in the here and now. As the poet philosopher Tagore, the greatest of modern Bengali writers, so poignantly proclaims:

> Faith is the bird
> that feels the light
> and sings while the
> dawn is still darkness.

The Spirit is like a gentle breeze, giving direction and breathing life into every event of our life and every word that we say. Gentle breezes seem to change direction frequently; the Spirit does that with us. We think we've got something going, a great inspiration has set us on what seems to be a life-long way, when suddenly we discover the Spirit anew, and another fascinating encounter with the divine occurs.

These changes are an important part of our spiritual development. They save us from settling into a pattern on which we might depend more than God himself. We come to the humble realization that the Spirit teaches and we *forever* are learners. Mystics are the Spirit's disciples. Seized in moments of divine encounter, we find ourselves once again in the poverty of learning.

And this is the security of the Spirit's lead.

Chapter Eight

Simply Love: Lessons from *The Cloud of Unknowing*

After we have spent many years of our lives praying, we may sense a strange dynamic coming into play. While we know that prayer is a good thing, somehow we feel that "saying" prayers is getting in the way of true union. We feel the need to just sit in God's presence in silence. Yet when we do, we get nervous or start thinking we should be *doing* something. So we try saying more prayers or different prayers, but nothing happens. Why is it that resting in the Spirit, which brings us peace, gets interrupted with the thought that "doing" is better than "being," or that "I'm just wasting my time"?

This is a critical juncture in our life of prayer—and a necessary one. It is a time of decision: to stay with God or to throw in the towel. It is time to find our spiritual center, allowing us to rise above the ebb and flow of "feelings" and spiritual "experience."

> It is much better to remain with God, apparently doing nothing in particular, than to make the grandest and most elaborate meditations.
>
> Abbot Chapman

About *The Cloud of Unknowing*

One of the oldest forms of prayer in our tradition comes to us from a fourteenth-century Englishman who well understood this struggle. His book, *The Cloud of Unknowing*, remains a popular treatise on the spiritual life that both challenges and comforts those on the way to a more intimate union with God.

The author of *The Cloud of Unknowing* remains anonymous, though many have attempted to name him. We do not know to what religious order he belonged, if, indeed, he was a monk. The oldest known manuscript of his work dates back to the fifteenth century. Since he seems to have known the works of Richard Rolle and since Walter Hilton knew him, historians conclude that he probably wrote in the late fourteenth century. Thus he belongs to the century of such spiritual greats as Julian of Norwich, Walter Hilton, Meister Eckhart, John Tauler, Jan van Ruysbroeck, Catherine of Siena, and Thomas à Kempis. His style indicates that he wrote in England's north-east Midlands.

Though *The Cloud of Unknowing* was written nearly two centuries before John of the Cross lived, there is a striking similarity in the two mystics' teachings. The mysticism of this book does not rest on any technique to induce contemplation and resolve the struggle we experience in moving toward God. The author speaks of God's desire: God's desire that we look at him and nothing more. God wants to act without restriction.

If God wants to act, then what do *we* do? *The Cloud of Unknowing* says, "Lift up your heart to God ... and mean God himself." This is not an intellectual fascination or imagination exercise. Though we can think many theological thoughts about God and imagine God's love for us, our thoughts and imaginings and the feelings they produce are not God. God is mystery, and we have to be satisfied to forget everything and to reach out to him with a simple, "naked" desire.

> I wish for you a tenacious desire to encounter God. For, the life that is given to us truly to live, the thing that we are called to do in the world for everyone that lives there, is the constant ebb and flow that, in every one of our acts, carries us from God and returns us to him.
>
> Madeleine Delbêl

Centering Prayer

Centering prayer, a contemporary recapturing of the prayer in *The Cloud of Unknowing*, is a very appealing form of prayer. Frs. Basil Pennington and Thomas Keating, both Trappist monks, popularized centering prayer because they saw the need for a simple, direct method that would bring *The Cloud of Unknowing* from the fourteenth century to our present day.

Centering prayer at first glance may seem like Zen or Yoga or transcendental meditation. But there is a distinct difference. While the Eastern forms of meditation use technique to produce states of consciousness, centering prayer *is* prayer. Those who "center" are on a journey to the loving heart of God, using one word (such as "God," "Christ," "Love") as a launching pad.

Centering prayer is simple; it presupposes that the love of God is the foundation of our being. This love created us and continually creates us anew. Without this love we simply would not be.

As you pray, you are professing your personal creed in God's sustaining and foundational love for you. You are not asking for anything particular, nor thinking about God or Jesus, nor formulating specific prayers, nor offering thanksgiving, nor making acts of contrition. You are, instead, consenting to the love that forever is, and silently declaring your faith that this love is trustworthy. It is all you need.

Let us begin.

1. *Choose a word.* This short word is a symbol of your intention, your willingness to allow God's presence to be active and fruitful within you. The word is like Mary's "yes." It is your consent, your awareness that you are allowing God's grace free rein within.

2. *Sit in a comfortable place and, if possible, close your eyes.* After a moment or two call to mind the word you have chosen. The word comes from the center of your being, used only to call your mind back when it wanders. The word should not be repeated over and over like a mantra or used like a hammer. It should be laid as gently as a feather on your consciousness.

3. *When you become aware of anything, return ever so gently to your word.* You will no doubt spend entire periods of prayer doing nothing more than calling your mind back. That is OK. That is part of the prayer. If you are faithful to centering prayer, you will find that this situation changes over time.

4. *At the end of the prayer period, remain in silence* for a few moments, open your eyes, and recite the Our Father.

The effects of centering prayer are revealed in the days and weeks and months that follow. Practice it at least twenty minutes every day. Or if you are able, it is even better to pray for twenty minutes in the morning and twenty minutes in the late afternoon.

Coming to Know the Unknowable

God is unknowable in the sense that he is beyond anything the human mind can conceive. St. Augustine affirmed, "If you have understood, then this is not God." St. John of the Cross wrote, "No idea can serve the intellect as a proximate means leading to God.... The intellect must advance by unknowing rather than by the desire to know, and by blinding itself and remaining in darkness" (*Ascent of Mount Carmel*, II, 9, 5). An ancient Christian mystic remarked, "Whoever sees nothing in prayer, sees God."

The important thing, then, is not the beautiful words we can say to God or our imagination of God, although both these things are good. In this prayer we simply love. The author of *The Cloud of Unknowing* speaks of a single word that can sum up our desire. This word becomes a dart that is sent up again and again to pierce the heavens and express our love, while at the same time it fills our minds and is our defense against distractions. By remaining faithful to this word, to which we come back again and again, we forget all else. God in his love will reveal himself because we open ourselves to his very personal gift.

It's important to remember that we cannot attain God by thinking of him, only by loving him. As we strive to give ourselves in love to God, as we remain still and patient with our "word," waiting in the darkness, we begin to be filled with the sense of awe and wonder that exists on the other side of the cloud of unknowing.

> God is over all things,
> under all things, outside all,
> within, but not enclosed,
> without, but not excluded,
> above, but not raised up,
> below, but not depressed,
> wholly above, presiding,
> wholly without, embracing,
> wholly within, filling.
>
> Hildevert of Lavardin
> eleventh century

The Gift of Dying to Self

So often we seek ourselves in prayer without realizing it! The warm fuzzy feelings, a "sense" of being holy, a magical assurance that we are pleasing God—these become the criteria for our measure of virtue. But our ways are not God's ways. All these "feelings" and "knowings" must be left behind for the cloud of unknowing, where we simply wait "with our word" for what seems to be nothing.

But in this nothing we find everything! We are weaned from the need to feel good about ourselves. We stop trying to score points with God, to assure ourselves of salvation. Instead we put faith in God's love for us, a love that eternally exists.

When we've truly forgotten ourselves—every once in awhile, even for just a split second—we experience the overflow of eternity into time, the flooding of our senses, the advance of God. But no sooner have we realized this than it is gone. We find that our God is elusive yet loving. He doesn't overwhelm us with his fullness.

The waiting in this form of contemplative prayer only seems painful and boring because we are not ready to experience the power, the light, and the love of God, who is giving himself to us. We can experience he who is Light only in his shadow, until we have been so purified that the split-second encounters with eternity transform us into Light.

This "death" of the self, though it feels like a terrible end, is indeed joyous. It takes us out of ourselves, and makes each self-offering an act of ecstatic love. There we abide in the One we love. This prayer is known also as "mystical marriage," because one becomes immersed totally in the Other. St. Paul explained it in these words: "It is no longer I who live but Christ who lives in me" (Gal 2:20).

> A contemplative has come to realize that if he possesses God
> he possesses all goodness and this is why he desires nothing in particular
> but only the good God himself.
> Let nothing except God hold sway in your mind and heart.
>
> *The Cloud of Unknowing*

Chapter Nine

Called to the Feast: Lessons From the Life of Venerable James Alberione

The Eucharistic celebration, the Eucharistic bread, and the Eucharistic assembly all share in the radical break with the expected. They introduce us to a contemplation that unites us *with* and *in* the body of the Lord as no other form of contemplative prayer can do. The richness and depth of the Mass give ample room for contemplative reflection.

Christ is the Messiah who saves us, the Lord who embraces us, the King who exercises dominion by serving us. He invites us to an eschatological feast in what are sometimes unexpected circumstances. We celebrate with people whom we barely know, with whom we may disagree, and who may have hurt us.

Together we listen to the Word, are challenged by it, convicted, and gradually transformed. Our separate lives are woven into one garment that clothes the world in the holiness of Christ. And as a group we pray for the world, a world that is missing what should be the most normal of things. Adoration, thanksgiving, and praise of God are our most complete way of being his creatures. What we read in the newspapers, which many of us accept as "the way the world is," is often the farthest thing from what God envisioned for creation. The Eucharistic celebration is the closest we can get to our *truest* self this side of heaven.

> To me nothing is so consoling, so piercing, so thrilling, so overcoming, as the Mass.... It is not a mere form of words—it is a great action, the greatest action that can be on earth. It is, not the invocation merely, but, if I dare use the word, the evocation of the Eternal.
>
> John Henry Cardinal Newman

Eucharistic Mystery

The entrance procession focuses our attention on the central mystery—both source and summit—of our life as the Church. To enter into the liturgy is to enter into the realm of God. The selected readings, assembled people, music, preaching, prayers, and Eucharist break us open in always-new ways.

The Eucharistic Prayer astounds us with the continued giving of life and mercy where death and fear abound. The bread and the wine become the Body and Blood of the One whose teaching, life, death, and resurrection confuse us yet still attract us. If we are honest, we *don't* understand how the poor are blessed or those who suffer are privileged, at least not when it's us. How could an ignominious death save us? How could our failures and setbacks bless us?

And yet, the bread and the wine that we lay upon the altar remind us of two things: first, we are called to a feast where the one we least expected to see there—perhaps one with whom we are not reconciled—has also been personally invited. Second, in the profound image of the professor of liturgy and author Aidan Kavanagh, we ourselves, if we are true to the food we receive, may find ourselves with broken bodies and spilled blood, lying on the altar. The Eucharist will cost us our lives, taken from us and returned to us through what we suffer and through the gospel decisions we embrace.

> Broken and distributed is the Lamb of God, Son of the Father, who is broken but not divided, ever eaten and never consumed, and who sanctifies those who participate.
>
> Byzantine Euchologion, Divine Liturgy,
> Formula at Fraction of Host
> (fifth to eighth century)
>
> Come, O my soul! Leave the world; come out of yourself; renounce yourself; and go to the God of the Eucharist. He has an abode in which to receive you; he longs for you; he wants to live with you, to live in you. Abide therefore in Jesus present in your heart; live in your heart; live in the goodness of Jesus Eucharistic.
>
> St. Peter Julian Eymard

Adoring the Presence of the Lord

In Communion we receive the Body and Blood of Christ. So simply, so humbly, he makes himself our food and our drink. He wants to be intimately united to us, to become one with us so we can become one with him.

The Eucharist is no simple symbol. It is truly Jesus Christ, crucified and risen. Just as he manifested himself in his body after the Resurrection—so real yet so subtle—this same sacred risen body is in the Eucharistic elements of bread and wine.

> Let us think of the Blessed Sacrament as the food of our souls; acting on us *without our ever knowing it.*
>
> Ronald Knox, *Window in the Wall*

In his Eucharistic presence, Christ remains mysteriously with us. Pope Paul VI writes, "To visit the Blessed Sacrament is ... a proof of gratitude, an expression of love, and a duty of adoration toward Christ our Lord." Spending time with Jesus in the Blessed Sacrament is a source of consolation and intimacy for our life in the Spirit. From the tabernacle, Jesus radiates his love and grace to the whole world, and in a special way to those who have come to adore him.

> In Holy Communion our hearts are the tabernacles of the Divinity. We should carefully guard the heart containing so precious a jewel.
>
> St. Elizabeth Ann Seton

About Venerable James Alberione

On November 26, 1971, journalists and news reporters scrambled to cover the death of an eighty-seven-year-old, frail, half-bent priest who, in his life, had been almost awkward in public and reluctant to speak of what he had done—Fr. James Alberione. Some said he was an apostle and a pioneer, others a saint and genius of our time. Always intent on scrutinizing the signs of the times, he had given to the Church new means by which to express itself: congregations of religious men, women, and lay cooperators who use the media for evangelization.

Venerable James Alberione often said, "From the tabernacle, everything; without the tabernacle, nothing." As a sixteen-year-old boy on "probation" in the seminary of Alba, Italy (six months earlier he had been asked to leave another seminary), James Alberione knew what it was like not to be trusted. He tried to fit into the order of the new seminary, but he still balked enough to be called "spitfire" by the other seminarians.

On December 31, 1900, James extended for four hours his prayer before the Blessed Sacrament in the Cathedral of Alba, along with many of the other seminarians. Yet for this seminarian who still felt himself to be a "misfit," Jesus was to break open the Word and the Eucharist and the world in a powerful way. James was ready.

While in adoration, James thought about the century that was just beginning. The words of Jesus, "Come to me all of you, and will refresh you" (see Mt 11:28), impressed themselves on his heart in a new way. He saw prophetically the needs of the people of the twentieth century, who would be catapulted into the communications revolution. He realized that the Eucharist is true communication: it is light, guidance, and refreshment; it is Way, Truth, and Life, able to illumine the needs of the people of this century and beyond.

Later, having founded congregations of priests and sisters to minister specifically in these "new" mission fields, Fr. James Alberione again met Jesus in a tangible way at the tabernacle. Jesus seemed to say to him, "Do not be afraid. I am with you. From the tabernacle, I want to cast light. Only be sorry for sin."

Eucharistic adoration became central to the lives of Venerable James Alberione and all his followers. The words of his vision are on the walls of all of the chapels of his Pauline family. He believed that visits to the Blessed Sacrament are meetings of our soul and of all our being with Jesus:

> It is the creature meeting his Creator; the disciple before the Divine Master; the patient with the Doctor of souls; the poor appealing to the Rich One; the thirsty drinking at the Font; the weak presenting himself to the Almighty; the tempted seeking a sure Refuge; the blind searching for the Light; the friend who goes to the True Friend; the lost sheep sought by the divine Shepherd; the heart led astray who finds the Way; the fool who finds Wisdom; the bride who finds the Spouse of the soul; the nothing who finds the All; the afflicted who finds the Consoler; the youth who finds life's meaning.

The Visit

Since the twelfth century, the Church has directed that the Eucharist be worshiped outside of Mass. Venerable Fr. James Alberione saw the hour of Eucharistic adoration as a "Visit" with Jesus—Truth, Supreme Goodness, and Life:

God as Truth

The Hebrew word for "truth" is not an intellectual proposition. It is instead a guarantee of the fidelity of God found ultimately in the person, life, death, and resurrection of Jesus Christ.

Therefore, begin your contemplation by adoring Jesus as

the fidelity of God. You will enter a world of safety and peace and be "realigned" with the truth of all God wants for you. Consider that "God would send his only Son to manifest his love for you" (see Jn 3:16). Open your heart and tell Jesus your troubles, fears, agonies, and crucifixions. Present to him decisions you need to make and dilemmas you are in. Jesus is at your disposal for as long as you want his attention.

Then pick up a book from which you can hear the wisdom of God: the Bible, especially the Gospels; a book of spiritual reading; the lives of the saints. Sit in the shade of Wisdom (Ws 6:12), or at the feet of Jesus as Mary did (see Lk 10:38-42), or in a crowd around him (see Mt 5); or kneel in the temple before the theophany, where the angels cry out, "Holy, holy, holy" (Is 6). Use your imagination if it assists you in entering the reading. Read short passages several times if repetition breaks open a passage in new ways for you.

God has said, "My thoughts are not your thoughts, neither are your ways my ways" (Is 55:8). Therefore, it is important to make acts of faith; to ask for the gifts of wisdom, understanding, and counsel; to seek the prudence of the saints, a deeper insight into our lives and the obligations we've assumed, and the grace to prepare our minds for the beatific vision.

As you visit with Jesus, you begin to see your situation, thoughts, lifestyle, and desires from different angles. You are called up and out of yourself. If you wish to conclude your reflection with a vocal prayer, pray the Creed, invoke the Holy Spirit, ask the intercession of the saints, or recite psalms.

God as Supreme Goodness

The second movement catches the imagination that longs for goodness, completeness, focus, authenticity, and purity of heart. Here the gift of wisdom begins to illumine life. Look for other gifts that have been given to you since you last visited Jesus. These can be in the form of consolations or challenges, or even buried in contradictions.

Examining your life in the light of wisdom is a joyful step in coming to the feast. The word "feast" appears almost fifty times in the New Testament. Life with Christ, our Christian reality, is a feast. We must want to be there, as Jesus pointed out in his parable of the wedding feast (see Mt 22:2-7). If you've asked to be excused from attending this divine party, there are many ways to express your sorrow: by praying an act of contrition, Psalm 51, the sorrowful mysteries of the rosary, or the stations of the cross; or by reflecting on the account of the passion, death, and resurrection of Christ in the Gospels.

God as Life

The third movement of the "Visit" honors God as Life, with and in Christ Jesus. Here you are left in silence—in adoration, in intercession, in reparation. What you have read or heard, the resonance of this within your conscience and life, spurs you to adore, to pray for yourself and others, to make reparation, to plead for grace and the gifts of the Holy Spirit. You may turn to the Mother of Jesus, Mary, and pray with her. Alberione also encouraged Marian prayer during this third movement of the "Visit."

As you grow in prayer, your prayer becomes simpler. Contemplation takes over more and more of the time you spend in adoration. Only a short passage of the Gospel may quiet your soul and bring you close to the heart of the Eucharistic Lord. An hour may pass in what seems but a few minutes. True conversation replaces method; and silent adoration teaches your heart, challenges your life, and sustains your soul. You will find yourself bringing everything before the Master, simply and with trust.

A Guide For Eucharistic Adoration

"The true hour of Eucharistic adoration, the true Visit," writes Venerable James Alberione, "is like the soul which pervades all the hours, occupations, thoughts, relations of our day. It is the lymph or vital current that influences everything and communicates its spirit even to the most ordinary things. It forms the spirituality that is lived and communicated. It forms the spirit of prayer which, when cultivated, transforms every work into prayer."

Before the Eucharistic Lord, Alberione would have you take as long as you need to become aware of how you are feeling. Call to mind what has happened in your life in the past day or week. Which events are shaping your life, affecting others in a serious way, or need to be looked at in the light of God's wisdom? Speak freely to Jesus of all that is in your heart.

The following three movements of the Visit to Jesus should be divided into more or less equal parts.

Truth

Read a passage from the Gospels or some other spiritual book. Make acts of faith and beg for the gift of wisdom. Reflect on how your spiritual reading can help you look at your life from new angles, from God's perspective. Ask for understanding, counsel, and prudence.

Goodness

Spend some time thanking God for all of salvation history, for his faithfulness to humankind in sending his Son to reconcile us and make us his children, for the many ways he has shown his fidelity and love to you in these past days. Reflect on how God has been revealing himself to you, how he has been awakening you to love him, follow him, give yourself to him more completely. Are there areas in your life that have not been healed by this love? Have you been afraid or resisted his requests? Express your sorrow, plan how you can be more responsive to God's presence, and ask God for his gracious help.

Life

Silence, contemplation, intercession, prayers of reparation, adoration—these are all forms of prayer that lead to a true communication between the Lord and you. God pumps his own life into your soul, at once softening and strengthening you, so that gradually he will be the one who lives in you, thinks in you, loves in you, reaches out to others in you.

Chapter Ten

Wrapped in the Heart of God: Lessons From the Life of Simone Weil

Contemplation: the word almost sounds like a warm, cozy cocoon. A silent space, dimly lit, with an open Bible and a candle is the image that comes to mind. But contemplation, if it is authentic, thrusts a person, more vulnerable than ever, into the reality God wishes to reveal to him or her.

Contemplation burns a heart clean, purifies vision, and unstops the ears. It awakens desires. It makes one aware, able to see what no one else may see and to hear who has been marginalized.

Through contemplation, God moves within our line of vision, as does our neighbor. The faces we see on television, those that grab our attention on front pages of newspapers, the persons we pass on the street, asking for a dime or a cup of coffee, wedge their way into our consciousness. The plight of our neighbor becomes our plight as well.

Our daily work becomes wrapped up in the heart of God's passionate love. Just as Jesus feeds us his own flesh and blood in the Eucharist, through work we break ourselves open in order to feed and serve others.

A wise person once said that there are three kinds of givers in this old world: the flint, the sponge, and the honeycomb. To get flint to give, you have to hammer at it and then it only yields sparks. Sponges you must squeeze, or else you get nothing. But the honeycomb—ah, the honeycomb drips its own sweetness.

Contemplation transforms us from being hard and stingy with others, or having to be forced into kindness, into cheerful people who give and give without ever being asked.

> The present form of the world passes away,
> and there remains only the joy of having used this world
> to establish God's rule here....
> When one has turned money, property, work in one's calling
> into service of others,
> then the joy of sharing
> and the feeling that all are one's family
> does not pass away.
>
> Oscar Romero, 1979
> *The Violence of Love*

About Simone Weil

Simone Weil was born in Paris in 1909. Her family was socially secure and "completely agnostic." Though her ancestors had been Jewish, the faith had quite disappeared in her immediate family.

Though comfort was what her family prized most, Simone never accepted this. While still a child, she refused to eat sugar since soldiers at the front were not able to get it, and the foundations of her spirituality were laid. World War I had brought into her life for the first time a sense of human misery, and her typical reaction was already set: to deny herself what the poor and the workers could not enjoy.

At fourteen she passed through the darkest spiritual crisis of her life, being pushed to the verge of suicide by her sense of her own unworthiness and an onslaught of migraine headaches that never left her. After receiving her degree in philosophy at the Sorbonne in 1931, Simone involved herself in the plight of unemployed workers. She started by joining the workers in their sports, picketing with them, and eating only the food allotted to the needy. She later took part in the Spanish War. In her political activity she was guided by the necessity of taking the side of the defeated and oppressed.

The crucial point of her conversion, though it happened many years later, started in these first forays into the lives of the workers. In Solesmes, while listening to Gregorian chant at the moment when her migraine was at its worst, she experienced the joy and bitterness of the passion of Christ. She wrote: "I felt, without being prepared for it (for I had never read the mystical writers) a presence more personal, more inaccessible to the senses and the imagination...." Even following this mystical experience, it took Simone five more years to allow herself to "say" conventional prayers. She resolved at that time to say the Our Father every day, and she did so with such intensity that apparently at each repetition, "Christ himself descended and took her."

Simone's mystical experiences did not separate her from her drive to immerse herself in the lives of the poor. She had a short stay in America, but the idea of living in such a secure country was intolerable for her. She returned to England, trying to reenter France, refusing to eat more than the rations allowed her countrymen in occupied territory. She died on August 24, 1943. Simone remained all her life on the threshold of the Catholic Church, awaiting an express command of God to be baptized.

Simone's life was one of intensity and contemplation, a spirituality that led her into the heart of the working and suffering people of her day. This identification with the poor and weak is at the heart of the Christian message. The following exercise is designed to help you more closely identify with this aspect of the contemplative heart.

❧

1. *In a quiet place, try to find stillness in your mind and heart.* Leave all worries and cares for a time, knowing you'll address them again, more vitalized, after this time of prayer.

2. *Breathe deeply.* Clear your mind. Recall the parable of the Good Samaritan, or take a few minutes to read it again in Luke, chapter 10.

   Creative attention calls us to create out of nothing. In the parable, the Samaritan saw the afflicted man lying on the side of the road. Out of his attentive gaze the Samaritan gave life where it was lacking. His love was equal to the person to whom he ministered.

3. *For a few minutes, close your eyes and relive the scene.* The victim, seriously wounded, lay on the side of the road. Those who passed by did so because their attention was elsewhere. The Samaritan's inner creativity recognized a living human

being. Out of the creativity of that moment the man's wounds were tended, he was brought to the nearest village, and his needs were provided for out of the Samaritan's own means.

4. *Now, in silence, take a few moments to consider your own creative awareness.* How do you react to others who seem to lie at the wayside: troublesome family members, a chronic complainer, people begging on the street, the cashier at the grocery store? Do you really *see* these people? Where is your attention when confronted with them? Is there a way to become creatively attentive to those who don't really "seem to exist" in everyday life?

5. *Open your heart.* Turn to Jesus, the Good Samaritan who is creatively attentive to you. Ask him for his eyes, his focus. Ask him to give you the capacity to be a life-giving friend to those who fall through the cracks, even if it means giving only a word or a smile when passing.

6. *Allow some quiet time to be attentive* to yourself, to be creatively aware of your deep need for God.

Enter Into the Suffering of Others

The ever-widening gap between the rich and the poor cries out to God for justice. Yet the plight of the poor can overwhelm us. We find unsettling the pain that confronts us in the homeless, the jobless, and the addicted. We might easily give a look of concern, a small service, a kindness. Thus we satisfy our need to feel good about ourselves—and then turn away.

> Lord, I'm not turning back. All that I have I now give to you. Ask me whatever; I never want to betray you.
>
> Carlo Maria Martini, S.J.

Simone Weil said, "To treat our neighbor who is in affliction with love is something like baptizing him." This sacramental love is worth far more than money and lasts longer than a cup of coffee. By letting our hearts ache with others' pain, feeling their sorrow within ourselves, these redemptive acts can become a baptism of compassion, pouring into them the life and love of the Trinity. In the words of Simone Weil, "In true love it is not we who love the afflicted in God, it is God in us who loves them."

Not only our hearts but also our bellies must ache. A conscious decision to break out of the consumer lifestyle, even in a small way, is a sacramental choice. Fasting one day a week, buying fewer clothes, simplifying one's furniture, refraining from obtaining the latest gadget on the market—these are often invisible choices, but they pump grace into our world, redeeming it from the inside out.

> Teach me your way of looking at people: as you glanced at Peter after his denial, as you penetrated the heart of the rich young man and the hearts of your disciples.
>
> Pedro Arrupe, S.J.

~

Chapter Eleven

The Courtesy of God: Lessons From the Life of Blessed Julian of Norwich

How intimately gentle God is with us. It is God's desire, according to Blessed Julian of Norwich, that we have the greatest security and happiness in God's love for us. The revelations of Julian, a fourteenth-century Englishwoman, recluse, and mystic, paint for us a portrait of a "courteous" God. This courtesy goes beyond what most of us perceive as a loving God. The extravagance of love expressed in her visions, or showings, speaks most directly to something our hearts can't believe, something we rarely experience on earth, something about ourselves that we can't get ourselves to believe.

God loves beyond any human being's power to love. God is pleased when we rejoice in that love, rather than worry over our misery. He wants us to rejoice in his secret purposes for our peace, purposes which are written into the verses of the Gospel, painted in the life, death, and resurrection of Jesus, explained in the parables, but purposes which we somehow can't quite get ourselves to bank our entire lives on. Even though we feel lack of peace, inner agony, strife, and endless turmoil, God is folding us in his goodness and meekness. We may feel bad about ourselves, but God does not. And that is the secret. Julian tries to get this across to us through a story from her visions.

There was a lord (who in the story is God) and a servant. The lord loved the servant, and the servant stood before his lord, ready to do his will. The lord sent him to a certain place. The servant not only went, but because of his love, jumped up suddenly and ran in great haste to do his lord's will. He immediately fell into a ravine and suffered great injury. The servant couldn't turn his head to see how near and kind his lord was. Instead he paid attention to his own misery. The servant was gravely bruised and in pain. No one bothered to help him.

Even in the ravine and in his misery, the servant was as good inwardly as when he stood before his lord. The lord gazed on him with great compassion, but also rejoiced because he would, through his grace, raise the servant from his fall. God then said to Julian that in just the same way, those that suffer falls in their service to him would be raised higher in their healing than they had been in their wholeness. God showed her that only pain blames and punishes us; the Lord who is instead most courteous comforts and assists. He always wears a cheerful expression for the soul, loving us, longing to raise us into everlasting bliss. Our attention to our misery often prevents us from seeing God as he is.

> Who can bind the soul that God sets free? Think of him, love him, and look at him. Never mind anything else. All shall be well.
>
> St. Elizabeth Ann Seton

About Julian of Norwich

Julian of Norwich was a mystic. Little is known of her, only that she lived as a recluse in a little room attached to a chapel in Norwich, England. Her total openness and submission to God's will attest to the truth of her experiences, which were recorded by a scribe, and are simply titled *Showings.*

Through her suffering, Julian conveyed a unique, gentle, and childlike relationship with God. Her "showings" draw the reader into a path of intimate union with Jesus in the Spirit. She was emphatic about her role as an intercessor between God and his people. Faithful to the teachings of the Church, she reflected the obedience, openness, and loyalty of a devoted daughter of Truth.

In her sixteen visions, Julian refers often to God's "courteousness." We appreciate courtesy from others. Can we imagine the Creator of heaven and earth, our first beginning and final end, Master and Ruler of time and space, being *courteous* to his frail and sinful creatures? Even when we choose to ignore our Maker, he doesn't intrude; he waits for an invitation. When we are ready and turn to him in need, he opens his arms wide to embrace us. Actually, his love has always been there for us.

And all shall be well,
yes, all shall be well,
all manner of things shall be well.
Blessed Julian of Norwich

Beginning contemplatives realize that one big adjustment needs to be made in their prayer life: stop striving, stop trying, stop worrying. Julian's famous quotation, above, should be a mantra for everyone who worries about doing the right thing in prayer, frets over failures, or anguishes over sins. God wants us to delight in him. That is all. He will make everything else "well" for us. This exercise is designed to set you on that path.

1. *If you have a portable, hands-free cassette or CD player, choose a favorite piece of instrumental music* to listen to while you walk.

2. *Start to walk slowly and reflectively.* Notice the beauty around you. "All shall be well." Notice the sunlight. "All shall be well." Take note of small animals that play on the ground. "All shall be well." If you pass others on the sidewalk, bless them silently. "All shall be well." Walk for fifteen minutes or so, with this blessing as a mantra, "All shall be well."

3. Returning home, *enter your special place of prayer.* Let your mind wander. If a worry arises, "all shall be well." If it is a resentment, "all shall be well." If it is a sin, "all shall be well." If it is a memory, "all shall be well."

4. *Picture Jesus on the cross.* Offer thanksgiving and praise for this work of love that surpasses anything for which we could have hoped.

5. *Picture God beside you.* Whether you are dirty or clean, your

life is rooted and grounded in Love. Because of God's goodness, which pervades and sustains your existence, he simply asks you to rejoice in who he is and forget who you are, losing yourself in your love for him. God longs to bring you into eternal bliss.

6. *Bring to mind your most compassionate image of God as well as your deepest worry.* Know that the Lord is with you. If you flee to him, he will comfort you and make you clean, secure, and safe. "All shall be well." End the time of prayer repeating, "All shall be well."

We Never Lose the Lord's Love

Blessed Julian of Norwich tells us that, even when we fall (and we see our fall, which we need to do), we never lose any of Jesus' love for us. And because we are tested through this failure of ours, we will have a particularly marvelous experience of love in eternity within the Trinity.

Instead of being frightened by our failures and sins, we must turn to God as to a mother and cry out for help: "Most gracious God, who are both a father and a mother to me, have mercy. I have made myself unlike you. I cannot make myself clean without your help and your grace." Jesus heals us over time, working in our souls what will give him the greatest glory for all eternity.

> He is our clothing. In his love he wraps and holds us. He enfolds us for love, and he will never let us go.
>
> Blessed Julian of Norwich

The Gift of Forgiveness

Can we begin to comprehend a love such as this? It is beyond our wildest expectations. Jesus will never pressure us to love him; he waits for us to be open. And when we make the slightest motion of wanting him in our life, he takes up residence in our souls as a true Friend, through his Holy Spirit. When we unite our wills to his most loving will, we find joy and peace. He is the Way that lovingly leads to the Father, he is our Redeemer and Lover, himself our living covenant with the Father!

This courteous God struggles to get through to us one simple message: "Delight in Me; rejoice in Me!" Spiritual people, especially, can become so entangled in their efforts to be more spiritual that they end up focusing on themselves and on their sins. In Julian's *Showings*, God says clearly, "Your sins are a matter of humility. But the deeds that I have done and will do are so unbelievable that I wish only that you would delight in Me."

Suffering is inevitable, part of our human condition. But our suffering can be united to the heart of Jesus, who knows what it means to be broken. With Jesus abiding in us, all is going to be well.

Jesus says, "I have overcome the world" (Jn 16:33). So the suffering due to evil in our lives can be turned into a valuable means of reconciliation between God and us and between us and our brothers and sisters. "All shall be well." At the judgment we will say, "Because things were the way they were, things were well. You have never made a mistake. May you, Lord, be blessed!"

We find refuge in the fact that we are loved and cared for by our God, even when we have failed him. He glories in a repentant heart. We need only turn to God and we are received into his gentle hands. Here we find the Trinity, Father, Son, and Holy Spirit, embracing us as a loving parent. Love, the inner life of the Trinity, flows into all creation, especially into each loving human being.

Our response to this love is prayer, which unites us deeply to God and his infinite love for us. We find prayer a way of life. Knowing and loving God become a full-time occupation. God himself makes the first move toward us; our response is that of a child who has absolute trust in the adult who is playfully tossing him into the air. Our trust becomes solid and our faith sure.

> God also showed [me] that sin will be no shame but an honor to man, for just as for every sin there is an answering pain in reality; so for every sin a bliss is given to the same soul. For the goodness of God never allows the soul that will come [to heaven] to sin without giving it a reward for suffering that sin. The sin suffered is made known without end, and the soul is blissfully restored by exceeding glories.
>
> Blessed Julian of Norwich
> *The Revelation of Divine Love*

~

PART III

COMMITMENT: THE TOTAL GIFT

Day after day, as we expose ourselves to the light of Jesus and his Word, something happens inside us. We begin to notice things God says to us, things we feel, things we hear, things we see around us. These things unsettle us and challenge us. And it may be years before we hear his words to us loud and clear: "We have grown to love each other. Come closer. Become like me."

Pope John XXIII, a deep contemplative, wrote, "I consider it a sign of great mercy shown me by the Lord Jesus that he continues to give me his peace, and even external signs of grace."

Nothing can get in the way of God's powerful, sweeping action in our lives once we have said yes to him. We may not feel his presence as a strong Lover, but he is little by little gathering the fragments of our lives together and transfiguring everything into mystery.

Jesus has taken us already where he wants us to go; he is our Way. As our Truth, he has assured us forever of the love that will uphold us; he is the absolute faithful covenant between the Father and us. He lifts up every corner of our day; he is our Life.

Chapter Twelve

Commit to Living Freely

Contemplation overflows into our lives, bringing us a new sense of *response*-ability. We learn from prayer and also from theology that God initiates all movement toward good in our lives. Through contemplation we become more and more sensitive to these inner movements. We begin to recognize more clearly where the Spirit of God is present and where the Spirit is absent.

Contemplation fine-tunes our awareness so that the Spirit's presence becomes more and more radiant. The choice to respond to the Spirit is always in our hands. We can refuse; we can feign ignorance; we can choose to be deaf. This deliberate non-responsiveness to the Spirit is the clearest way to grasp the nature of sin in our daily lives. Our refusals often lead to actions that violate the law of God and communion with his people, as well as our vocation to love and service.

This non-responsiveness penetrates the marrow of our days more completely than does the vague list of sins we may look over before confession. Perhaps the drop we have seen in the reception of the sacrament of penance is precisely because our sense of the Spirit's direction in our lives has weakened.

We can also freely choose to respond to the Spirit's gentle voice. Contemplation—in which we practice listening to the voice of the Spirit of God—reveals to us our total dependence on God. The source of all our goodness is *not* ourselves, our willpower to do good, or our strength based on our health. We wait upon the Spirit.

1. *Make a list of your daily activities.* Choose a day and as you go through each activity, observe whether or not you are aware of being led by the Spirit.
    - Do you start the day with a time of silent contemplation, however short?
    - Do you stop to offer a prayer before making a decision?
    - Is driving time simply a mindless exercise, or are you aware of soaking in the Spirit's peace?
    - Do you feel God with you as you begin an activity? Are there some activities in which you feel this and others in which you don't? Try for a few days to notice your awareness of the Spirit's presence and activity.

2. *For a week, try starting each day with a five-minute period of contemplation.* If you are very busy, do it while you're drinking coffee, or get up five minutes earlier. Open yourself to the Spirit and ask for guidance during the day.

3. *Choose two activities of a typical day in which you especially wish to follow the Spirit's lead.* Picture the activity, what usually happens in the course of it, what you would like to change, how you would like to approach it differently, what you need. Ask the Spirit to come into that activity with you, in you, and through you. At the end of each day review those two activities, and see if you were aware of the Spirit's presence and where the Spirit was leading.

4. *Look at the decisions you made in those activities and see the results of those decisions.* By these results you will know if the decision was made according to the Spirit or some other drive, compulsion, or temptation. You might keep track of the decisions and their results on one side of a piece of paper, and on the other side take note of what prompted you. The goal of this exercise is simply to become more aware.

Life in the Spirit

Philosophers such as Gabriel Marcel have warned us that our world today turns each of us into a commodity, a number, a statistic, a role. As commodities, we are bought and sold to advertisers. The number of eyes viewing a program or an Internet page determines its worth.

Advertising appeals to our compulsions.

"You need this."

"Try it and get a free gift!"

"Make a six-digit income in one month from your home without even trying."

Click here, watch that, check out something else. These enticements appeal to desires within us.

Is the Spirit behind those decisions to "click," "watch," "check out"? Maybe, but maybe not. Only you know the difference—at first. Your pocketbook, charge account, family, and friends will be able to tell the difference eventually. "Thus you will know them by their fruits" (Mt 7:20).

> The rich man ... who held his things lightly and did not let them nestle in his heart, who was a channel and not a cistern ... (in heaven sits) side by side with the man who accepted, not hated, his poverty. Each will say, "I am free."
>
> George MacDonald

It is possible to live freely in a world that hands us over to judgment, evaluation, measurement, and commerce. We can do so if we live with the freedom of the Spirit. When we lift ourselves above or swim deeply below the desires to buy, get ahead, be number one, we live in the power of the Spirit.

It is the Spirit of God who makes us children of the Father and sets us free. He will speak and act in us, through us, and for us. Jesus said, "When they bring you to trial and deliver you up, do not be anxious beforehand what you are to say; but say whatever is given you in that hour, for it is not you who speak, but the Holy Spirit" (Mk 13:11).

> Lord, you are my Lover, it is you whom I desire. You flow through my body like a stream, you shine on my face like the sun. Let me be your reflection.
>
> St. Mechthildis of Magdeburg

Chapter Thirteen

Commit to Reconciliation

Joan Pierce was a grandmother whose heart was broken. She had only once seen her granddaughter (on her first birthday), and even then had been asked to leave after unpleasant words had been exchanged. She had never held her grandson.

Her son Andrew had married a woman whom she herself had introduced to him. What had started as a close bond had ended in a painful break, when Andrew and his young wife had moved away. For reasons Joan did not entirely understand, her daughter-in-law, Christina, wouldn't speak to Joan and seemed to pit Andrew against his mother. Joan remembered birthdays and sent Christmas cards, but received no response for several years.

Five years to the day after he had asked his mother to leave his house, Andrew decided to give himself a birthday present, one that would mean more to him than a new shirt or a dirt bike. He called his mother. For several hours they spoke together in a tense but hopeful conversation.

Reconciliation does not come easily to humans. All of us have memories of unsettled pain, angry feuds, and silent standoffs. Only the incomprehensible imagination of the Suffering Servant of Yahweh could offer us the redeeming gift of reconciliation.

Jesus—a solitary figure, vulnerable and afraid, lifted up on a mound of dirt called Calvary—allowed his very life to be destroyed by the hatred and insecurity of others. He willingly remained defenseless, open, gentle, and poor. The Lion of Judah offered himself as a Lamb of sacrifice. Light succumbed confidently to darkness and defeat.

How could he not strike out in self-defense, asserting his rights, demanding respect? Where were the ones he had healed, forgiven, raised from the dead? Where were his closest friends and followers? A life of gentleness and love seemed to be ending, torn apart in the chaos of hurt, hate, and misunderstanding.

Jesus chose to be powerless, to absorb the violence, to surrender to pain, to death, to non-meaning. This seems impossible for us. Yet Jesus says, "Follow me."

> You, O eternal Trinity, are a deep sea, into which the more I enter the more I find, and the more I find the more I seek.
>
> St. Catherine of Siena

Reconciliation is a many-layered process. Even when it is achieved, pain can resurface and memories can mar. From the charred timber of our burned relationships, however, lovely flowers can bloom.

Settle down to prayer, reflecting upon a painful incident. Remember that God is with you, holding and protecting you as you bring this incident to him in prayer. You may find it helpful to do one of the following:

1. *Formulate in your journal the heart of the issue.* Describe in detail the context, background, and your own feelings about the situation. How did the situation begin? Who was involved? How did you feel then? How do you feel now? What do you need the Lord's help with?

   Then wait quietly for whatever comes to mind. An image, a feeling, a memory or a thought, even a Scripture verse, might present itself. Record whatever bubbles up from within you, without judgment. Talk to the Lord and listen to what he has to say about the situation. Record the dialogue as it happens.

2. *Allow yourself to feel.* Hurt feelings normally arise from painful situations, angry feelings from unjust ones. Feelings are indicators that something about a situation needs to be reflected upon and resolved. Feelings are of the heart; don't try to control them with your head. These feelings, no matter how deep they seem, eventually give way to deeper feelings that are more telling than the initial reaction.

3. *Pray for Christ's healing.* Choose a Gospel passage in which Jesus forgives someone, such as the paralytic (see Lk 5:18-26), the woman accused of adultery (see Jn 8:3-11), or Peter after his triple betrayal (see Jn 21:15-19). Relax and settle into God's presence, asking for the gift of compassion, or for healing in the particular area of your life that needs reconciliation. Read the passage aloud several times, allowing half a minute between each reading. Then set the Bible aside, and imagine yourself there with Jesus. Stay alert to the Spirit, drifting in and out of the scene as he invites. Do not moralize or make applications; simply lose yourself

in the persons and words of the scene itself. Then give thanks to the Lord for his presence to you during this time.

4. *Release your struggle to forgive into God's hands.* Forgiveness and reconciliation are difficult. You may not be at a point where you are able to forgive. That is all right. Put into God's hands your *desire* to forgive. That is enough. Sit contemplatively each day, repeatedly entrusting this desire to God. He will bring you into his forgiveness in his own time.

Being Ready to Change

On the cross, Jesus could remain defenseless because he knew his Father loved him. He had listened to and was certain of his Father's Word to him. He did not need to grasp status, possessions, or dignity. These he could relinquish because his Father would never stop loving him. He was sure of that.

He tells us, "As the Father has loved me, so I have loved you" (Jn 15:9). And, "Greater love has no man than this, that a man lay down his life for his friends. You are my friends" (Jn 15:13-14). Jesus showed us the way to true love: having a forgiving heart. We are called to be a forgiving people.

It is not easy. We can think of umpteen times when we've been sinned against. Parent and child, spouse and in-law, employer and employee, student and teacher, and even friend and friend: countless stories of wounds opened, hearts broken. But as followers of Christ, we are asked to be like him, reconciled in our lives with God and with one another.

Forgiving another person means that we ourselves must be ready to change. The words may be easy to say: "I forgive you."

They seem to be an almost condescending wave of a magic wand, clearing the air and bestowing a fairy-godmother state of bliss on a relationship. But people can't relate to fairy godmothers.

They *can* relate to struggling people like themselves. Being ready to forgive, therefore, means realizing that behind the other person's offensive or socially problematic behavior is a cry asking to be heard, a pain from the past not dealt with, or a statement about the present not articulated. Forgiveness means I need to hear what is *not* being said, opening myself up to that truth. I need to allow the other person into my heart. It means acknowledging my own selfishness, anger, bitterness, negative attitudes, and ways of thinking, and turning to Jesus to ask forgiveness.

> Be at peace with your own soul; then heaven and earth will be at peace with you.... The ladder that leads to the kingdom is hidden within your own soul. Flee from sin, dive into yourself, and in your soul you will discover the stairs by which to ascend.
>
> St. Isaac the Syrian

Revealing God's Love

Jesus made the Father's love something we could see and touch. Similarly, we become love for one another. We are not automatic channels conducting the Father's love to those around us; that would be too clean and neat. No. The Father's love gets mixed up in our lives, and that can be messy.

His love takes on *our* eyes, *our* ears, *our* voices. His love abiding in us takes on *our* mannerisms, *our* tone of voice, *our* attitudes. Every word we say, everything we do, all that we are, can reveal his love. The Father does not need perfection; he can work through our brokenness. His power in us is so great that even in our weakness he gives himself to another. Our pain reveals his glory. Receiving his forgiveness helps us become gentler with others.

Letting go of hurt can be a lifetime work, especially if we've been manipulated or abused. Some pain will never go away completely. Often it is necessary to set boundaries on certain behaviors. We don't condone what is sinful. However, we can look at the other as a *person,* one weak like ourselves, someone who needs God's forgiveness and ours, too. "We love the sinner but hate the sin." By our generous act of loving we can help another turn to God for forgiveness.

> Forgiveness is part of the treasure you need to craft your falcon wings and return to your true realm of divine freedom.
>
> Hafiz

Chapter Fourteen

Commit to Carrying Christ's Cross

The cross: it is the privilege of the Christian, a stumbling block to the world. Inherent in our baptism, infallible in its coming, incalculable in its graces, the cross enters all our lives sooner or later. Its coming will make or break us. It often makes us only *after* breaking us.

What is your cross? It may be the loss of a job, the death of a parent, the illness of a child, cancer, natural disaster, an accident or misunderstanding, loneliness, or chronic pain. When it appears it is never *our* cross, though it is individually tailored to us. It is always the cross of Christ.

Fifteen years ago I was admitted to routine outpatient surgery on my foot and suffered a stroke during or after the operation. I was twenty-one. A reaction to anesthesia? A mistake? Who will ever know? The physical, mental, and emotional havoc it brought into my life is still a cross I carry.

When I asked a priest friend of mine, "Why me?" he answered, "Why *not* you?" I spent many months, even years, in anger. I hated the cross and rejected all it stood for. I sat long in the darkness reading the Book of Consolation in Isaiah (chapters 40-66) as a sheer act of faith. I sought everywhere for an answer to the question of suffering.

In my best moments I came to realize, deep within me, that there is no answer. I no longer need to ask the question: it makes no sense, and asking it only blocks resurrection. I wrestle with the cross till I fall in love with the Crucified and embrace his death in order to experience his resurrection.

The bad things that happen to us make us feel, at times, that we are at the mercy of fate. Life seems meaningless, and a quiet cynicism invades our attitude. Without the mystery of the cross, life would be incomprehensible.

> The most helpful discovery of today has been that right in the midst of my sorrows there is always room for joy. Joy and sorrow are sisters; they live in the same house.
>
> Macrina Wiederkehr

Often we cannot face the cross directly in prayer. Even Jesus prayed to his Father, "Let this cup pass from me" (Mt 26:39). We need to be patient and respectful with ourselves when still in shock over bad news, a betrayal, an unjust situation, or whatever form the cross takes in our life.

Imagine yourself at the moment of death. Then again, picture your funeral and what others are recalling of you. See yourself before all the angels and saints and God himself. Spend some time daily distancing yourself emotionally from the cross present in your life right now.

When you are ready, pick up the Scriptures, the lives of the saints, or another book. Let God freely speak to your situation. When you find a passage particularly meaningful to you, stay there for several days in your prayer.

Ask yourself, at the point of death, what would you wish you had done? You don't need to formulate an answer; the question, instead, will direct your life. The cross will enrich you as a person if you can sit with its mystery. You have only to wait and see.

In *His* Hope Is Our Hope

The cross can be an experience of utter darkness: absolute abandonment, the emptiness that nothing can fill. And yet, the fact that another has gone before us in the darkness gives us a glimpse of the gray hope of eventual day. Jesus, utterly abandoned by the Father in his time of need, turns us to face the darkness. It is not darkness devoid of everything; it is a darkness Another has embraced for our sake.

> In our sleep, pain that cannot forget
> falls drop by drop upon the heart
> and in our own despair, against our will,
> comes wisdom through the awful grace of God.
>
> Aeschylus

Nothing is beyond the suffering of Jesus. He dwells in our darkness—not inert and careless but as one who feels it all: the emptiness, the gloom, the despair.

Rachael was in her mid-forties, a wife and mom. Her strong sense of family came second only to her faith. Her world shattered one July evening several years ago when her husband of twenty-two years told her that he was being investigated for pedophilia. Tom also told her there was some truth to the allegations.

In the ensuing months the terrible hurt almost immobilized Rachael. She bottled her own anger but lashed out when she saw the pain her teenage son and daughter experienced.

She knew that God was asking something, perhaps testing something, but she didn't know what it was. Even without this answer, however, she knew she would not turn her back on God. Only one thing sustained her through the years of anguish that followed: knowing that God's answers to her prayers would arrive—not in her time but in *his.*

Rachael had to learn that accepting help was more difficult than giving it, as family and friends rallied to support her during her husband's arrest, investigation, and court proceedings. She knew that God had sent these "angel friends," as she calls them, to help her carry her cross. They were her Simon of Cyrene as the story made headlines, not only in their small-town newspaper and television but in news broadcasts across a dozen states.

For many months Rachael's life seemed like a long, dark tunnel with no light at the end. The proceedings devastated her financially and drained her emotionally, physically, and spiritually. Sometimes a glimmer of light turned out to be only another locomotive steaming through the tunnel, running her over.

Prayer and time heal. Rachael's daily rosary has brought her consolation and revelation. She says that life is like the rosary: a third is joyful, a third sorrowful, and a third glorious. She feels her many blessings are joyful and glorious.

Rachael's life has come a full and blessed circle. By the grace of God, she and her children have learned that they are survivors. Now independent twenty-somethings, the children have begun careers and are very close as a family. Rachael has found again her sense of wholeness, along with a new sense of direction and strength.

When her life is challenged with future crosses, Rachael will not ask God "Why?" or "Why me?" She will carry the cross because she has seen that there is a glorious resurrection, and beyond that an ascension as well.

Praying in the Darkness

The cross can often lead to the darkness of depression, more so today in a world that is ruthless and often doesn't allow a second chance. Depression, however, is not the last word. At these times we need to turn to people who love and care for us: a trusted friend, family member, parish priest, therapist, or doctor. When we reach out we discover the many people who love us, though we often can't believe in their love or feel ourselves to be lovable. The challenge is moving beyond those feelings in order to find ways to be connected. Though the darkness is deep, love is around us like a vibrant light.

When we shoulder the cross, we may not be able to understand. We may struggle to accept. We may feel our prayer lacks connection with God or anyone else. I know people who have gone three, five, ten years without "praying," though they faithfully adhered to a time set aside for contemplation. All there was, was a haunting darkness. Loneliness, boredom, frustration, anger. Contemplation? Even here.

Recognizing this agony of the void calls the person to be present to the now—even if the now is darkness. God is in that void—the Father hearing the prayer-agony of his only Son, "My God, my God, why have you forsaken me?" To be present to that agony, and to know that Jesus is in that agony with us and for us, is contemplation, even when no prayer or act of love passes through our hearts. His abiding love is deep within, never forsaking us. Contemplation calls us where prayer escapes us or even makes us angry. There we are alone in the void with the Son of God—both of us keeping silent.

> Lord, my soul is so dry that by itself it cannot pray; yet you can squeeze from it the juice of a thousand prayers.
>
> Guigo the Carthusian

For one friend who was faithful to this contemplation of silence, there was eventually a turning point. Almost imperceptibly something seemed to change, like a very slow sunrise. Meeting her after years of struggling with prayer, of thinking she hadn't prayed, I found that she possessed a prayerful heart of strength, depth, and compassion. She had experienced a mystery of the life of Christ that many never do. She had suffered the passion to the bitter end, and she had been esurrected gloriously.

Chapter Fifteen

Commit in the Dark Nights

Contemplation is prayer, but as we have seen, it is also life. In previous chapters we have taken up the integration of our life into our prayer. As the Spirit works in us and God takes over, another step of integration takes place. Prayer and life and desire are swept up into one goal: to be totally God's.

> Out of love Jesus took us to himself and gave his life's blood for us—he gave his body for our body, his soul for our soul.
>
> St. Clement

There is a long path to this point of full union, when all we want is what God wants. Even after many years of contemplative prayer, we can be but beginners in this relationship. Though we may have rooted out obvious sin from our lives, certain faults still hold back our growth toward full union with God.

Looking More Closely

Self-knowledge is absolutely necessary in order to know God. The Spirit gradually reveals to us deeper and deeper layers of our life. Some of what we see is our old nature, part of which can be transformed only through suffering and dark nights.

Persons who pursue contemplation often develop a certain self-satisfaction and vanity about their spirituality, which is a form of spiritual pride. They compare themselves with others, making sure that their feats of fervor take place where others can stand in awe. They are waiting for the rest of the spiritually insensitive world to discover their sanctity. By themselves they can usually mortify obvious expressions of self-adulation and self-display. But, as Barbara Dent says in *My Only Friend Is Darkness*, "the roots of fascination with our own unique splendor and consequent denigration of others remain undisturbed.... Only the celestial surgeon is competent to undertake such operations, and he does so in the passive purgations."

> From the cowardice that dare not face new truth, from the laziness that is contented with half truth, from the arrogance that thinks it knows all truth, Good Lord, deliver me.
>
> Prayer from Kenya

Spiritual avarice attaches itself to the accidents rather than the substance of devotion. People read book after book, try method after method, go from director to director, never satisfied that they are getting anywhere fast enough. They cannot believe that prayer can be so boring. They become depressed when they do not receive consolations in prayer and can even manufacture feelings of devotion, tears, sighs, and angelic gazes in order to fill their emotional need.

Those at this stage no longer commit deliberate sins of bodily sensuality. However, they can find themselves frustrated with uprisings of sensual thoughts, images, impulses, and rebellions even at prayer. They can be tempted to discouragement, to give up prayer altogether. They can also find themselves looking for pleasure for its own sake, often rationalizing their self-indulgence and weakening their wills.

They can find themselves at times growing bitter, resentful, angry, disappointed, or annoyed when they realize they have not become saints instantaneously and when prayer does not yield the expected joy. Irritation with others' failures quickly follows, along with pointing fingers when they find others not as "far along" as they should be.

Who can really measure "progress"? Doesn't God know where we are going and how we are going to get there much better than we do? We must learn to wait with trust and confidence in the goodness of the Lord.

> Because the virtues you have in mind do not shine in your neighbor, do not think that your neighbor will not be precious in God's sight for reasons that you have not in mind.
>
> St. John of the Cross

The Night of Faith

We have come as far as we can come on our own. At this time we must be lifted up and taken over a mighty chasm to the other side, where we are placed in the dark, in a desert, without a map, and without a guide. In progressive nights of faith, God begins to give himself to us in a more direct way and to purge us of the roots of sin.

There are three signs by which we can know if we have entered the passive night of the senses.

We are not getting out of prayer what we used to. For a considerable period of time, we have received no pleasure or consolation or sense of achievement from our relationship with God, our prayer, or our work for him. We find it impossible to meditate, but at the same time we find ourselves drawn to sitting quietly in God's presence, doing nothing.

Nothing gives us a sense of satisfaction. Our jobs, our personal relationships, and our accomplishments bring only temporary and minor joy, if anything at all. We realize only God can satisfy us.

We sense this state is not due to sinful habits, illness, or fatigue. At the same time, we wonder if we are falling short of what God wants of us. Have *we* caused this painful situation in which God seems absent? Has our lack of perseverance caused the emptiness? We desire God and continually watch ourselves for signs of backsliding.

Usually, it is best to discern these signs with the help of a director or someone else who knows us well. (See chapter 18 for more on spiritual direction.)

In the wine cellar
I drank of my Beloved, and,
when I went abroad
through all this valley,
I no longer knew anything,
and I loved the herd that I was following.
There he gave me his breast;
there he taught me a sweet and living knowledge;
and I gave myself to him,

keeping nothing back;
there I promised to be his bride.

St. John of the Cross

❧

At this point in contemplation, one feels like a train that has pulled to a stop. The doors of all the cars have been opened. Everything is dark within, dark and waiting. The power of the engines has been shut off. The dust around the tracks settles. Now is the time when the Divine Master himself will enter each car, turn on the lights, and begin to sweep around what is in them. As he brings his light, he and we see the dirt within. As long as we don't resist his searching and his sweeping, he is not disturbed by anything he finds. He is not there to fix what he finds. He will heal it in his own way. Honesty and humility are all the Master asks as he goes about his work.

Spend an hour opening the doors and letting in the Master. Consciously lower the anxiety that comes from not "getting ahead" or "becoming holy." Allow Jesus to lead you into each car, each area of your life. See with him whatever he shows you. It is not time to analyze, defend, or repudiate what you find. Instead, let the Master show you and take over the work of prayer and growth in you.

The train will never start again. It has arrived at its destination. Now the Master is taking over the cars as his own abode and creating there the garden of his delight. What you shall be will be entirely his work and his gift created over the years, while you see mainly what he is cleaning out and sweeping away. Spend as much time as you can with Jesus.

God at Work

St. John of the Cross assures us that though this state feels painful to us, it is actually the result of God's beginning to feed the soul secretly with contemplation. God's giving himself as Light overpowers our soul, which is still filled with darkness. We see and feel the darkness rather than the Light. God is at work in us and producing effects that we cannot understand or control. He is weaning us from the familiar and introducing us to the new and incomprehensible. We find ourselves compelled to seek silence and solitude, yet when we are there we do not feel the presence of the One we have sought.

> I do not stay there [at prayer] for my own sake, but for God's. I go to see God because it delights him, because he likes to see me.
>
> St. Thérèse of Lisieux

During this time we fear we have relaxed into lukewarmness, that our inability to pray means that we are wasting our time at prayer, or that God is punishing us for something. We need to calm this unrest, make an act of faith, and stay in the pain-filled silence without question or disturbance. A good director can be of great help at this time. An inexperienced director, however, might do harm by encouraging a person to return to meditating in order to feel the presence of God.

At this stage, our criticizing and pompous ideas for ourselves have dropped out of mind. The publican's prayer becomes ours: "God, be merciful to me a sinner" (Lk 18:13). We begin to become truly humble, obedient, and meek, allowing our desires to be drawn by the desires of God.

Once we have entered the night of faith, we continue in it until death, for we can only really know God in this world through faith. These nights persist also because, no matter how holy we become, we are still tempted, we still fall, involuntary imperfections still show up, and virtues need to be developed. Above all, we can always grow in love.

God's Desire

The dark nights will become part of the life of one who wishes to be all God's. As we cease to struggle, God himself goes where we cannot. He often delves deep into the psyche and, like an excavator, tears up the pavement, the pipes, the tunnels, the foundation, and everything else as he works. But as he works he tells us to trust that he knows what he is doing.

> When our strings are well-tuned God can spontaneously play on our soul. And we should aim at nothing more than this: to stretch out toward and be tuned by God.
>
> Hans Urs von Balthasar

God will lead us from where we think we know, to where we don't know, to where we hand over all knowing. We will be invited to faith in God, who is working within us, burning away every desire, thought, and plan that is not his own. We will find cherished ones moving away, jobs lost, ideals broken. We may encounter financial devastation, reversal of plans, complete failure.

These hardships are not without purpose. God is trying to get us to a place where we have no assurance within ourselves that all is well, a state where no clear path lies ahead, a space of spiritual inadequacy where we must turn to him in trust. God made us for no other reason than to give himself to us. He wants us to let him love us. He longs for our deep choice of him, our total orientation to him. He wants to pour himself out on us in everlasting joy.

PART IV

PERSEVERANCE: PRELUDE TO TRANSFORMATION

Many people are invited to the table of God's love. Some of these enter seriously into the period of engagement, with the joys and challenges that sustained periods of contemplation bring. Of these, fewer commit themselves seriously to a rhythm and a vision of contemplation that integrates their entire being—their relationships and experiences, their successes and failures, their crosses and depressions, as well as their involvement in the technological matrix and pop culture that surround them.

Even fewer persevere. Why? I believe simply that, despite the thousands of books on spirituality that stock the shelves of stores and libraries, the mystical life still remains something "outside" of our life. Many chapters on the degrees of prayer or the psychological effects of the illuminative way leave out the extremely important reality that "I need only allow God to love me, pray in me, transform me." Letting go is one of the hardest things for us to do: not do it myself, not plan it myself, not schedule it in.

We often miss telltale signs of God's work. We slide or crawl through experiences without realizing what they could be if we put into the mix a little faith. "Mystical contemplation" makes us think of cloistered nuns; we feel it is incompatible with "real life," as though we must kiss it good-bye when wrestling three kids into the car. We can get lost in the noise, afraid of the shuffle, taken for a ride by the consciousness created by our technological world, all the time missing heaven in our souls.

Having said that, any reader who has persevered to this point, reading and praying, *is* ready to go on. Perseverance is within reach.

In a relationship, the years of perseverance follow the first years of active commitment. They are long years that move us gently toward our senior years—of wisdom, gentleness, and peace. In a prayer relationship, with God as our Love, the years of perseverance slowly slip us into a passive state in which God takes over more and more. We are the receivers, and God is the active Partner.

This section of the book is not just for those who have attained a "higher stage" of contemplation. These are not pages to be read in the future, once everything that has come before has been practiced perfectly. Rather, this part outlines the action of God underlying everything that has gone before and points the way to the future.

The worst thing we can do is try to find out where we are in a dynamic process, a process that in reality ebbs and flows uniquely with the ebb and flow of each individual life. Instead, we try to understand how to go about the simple yet so complex response of allowing God to love us, live in us, transform us, while at the same time relinquishing our need to be spiritually "finished" at any time.

The clearest historical expression of the way God is with us as we are being transformed through contemplation can be found in the forty days between the Resurrection and the Ascension. There the Eternal allowed himself to be drawn into time. He encountered his disciples, ate with them, touched them, spoke to them. The following chapters, which spotlight moments within this forty-day span, recapture what has been said in these pages and offer an invitation to continue on this path until heaven opens for us the everlasting reward of a life of contemplation.

Chapter Sixteen

Keep Walking

When our hearts are transformed in vibrant love and Christianity beats strongly within us, it is essential to keep up the rhythm of practices we began many pages, months, or years ago. The practices may have matured or simplified, but the human condition and psyche demand the constant rhythm created by practice.

There is no neutral ground. Either we go forward or backward. Practice keeps us walking, even if we lose the path or it offers steep climbs or unhappy twists. In the end we find that what we have achieved is an awareness of what we already had. For all that we "achieve" is the awareness of God's gift, which we now more graciously long for and receive.

After the Resurrection, Peter and the apostles went back to fishing (see Jn 21:3ff). In a way, you could say, they gave up their "practice" of waiting with faith. The death of the Master, the confusion of the reports of Jesus' missing body, and the strain of waiting for Jesus to reappear were too much for them. They returned to the past. And they caught nothing.

Not only did the apostles give up their practice; even their understanding of their identity was, for a night, weakened. They took on their former role as fishermen, and their reality as "apostles" was obscured.

In the morning hours, however, Jesus broke into their world once more. John, the mystic, saw him first and pointed him out. Peter, forever full of color and texture, jumped into the water and got himself to shore, where Jesus already had breakfast on the fire. The apostles needed no clarification; they knew it was the Lord. Jesus recalled them to the practices: to the Eucharist, to fellowship with each other built around his presence, to community. He pulled the community of apostles back together, and they never again returned to fishing.

> Since we are never determined, but full of human prudence and a thousand fears, you, consequently, my God, do not do your marvelous and great works. Who is more fond than you of giving ... when there is someone open to receive?
>
> St. Teresa of Avila

Were we to return to our lives before we began the rhythm of contemplative prayer, Jesus would again break in, and we would know it was he. Jesus rearranges our mental constructs. He teaches us through what he accomplishes in our midst. He takes us back with simple questions about our love for him. He restores us in the community and in our practice. And as he revealed to the apostles the community they already were, he reveals to us in an instant what we already are, drawing our hearts to everything we really want to be.

This is the kind of Friend
You are—
Without making me realize
My soul's anguished history,
You slip into my house at night,
You silently carry off

All my suffering and sordid past
In Your beautiful
Hands.

Hafiz

Practice mellows the ego. Practice makes us gentle and rounds the corners that harshly tear at us. Practice makes the changing continue, so that we walk from freedom to freedom, beauty to beauty, love to love.

Reflect on the experiences that have surfaced while using the prayer exercises in this book. Identify three forms of prayer that brought you the greatest peace and growth.

- ____
- ____
- ____

What potential obstacles do you see that could prevent you from practicing these prayer forms?

- ____
- ____
- ____

Conversely, what resources do you have available to you that can help you delve more deeply into the practice of these prayer forms?

- ____
- ____
- ____

After reading this book, what do you think would be some signs that you are experiencing spiritual growth as a result of practicing these prayer forms each day? What do you sense God is asking of you?

- ______________________________
- ______________________________
- ______________________________

Chapter Seventeen

Practice a Life of Prayer

The Pilgrim's Tale recounts the spiritual journeys and adventures of one person who wanted to take seriously St. Paul's advice to "pray unceasingly." The pilgrim visited churches and diligently listened to homilies on this subject. Each discourse, however, left him more confused than before. The explanations were mediocre, self-contradictory, and often untrue to Scripture. Finally he met a monk who agreed to teach him what St. Paul meant by attending always to God.

The monk taught him the Jesus Prayer. He instructed him, "Sit in silence. Bend your head, and close your eyes. Breathe quietly. With your imagination, look within your heart. Carry your thoughts from your head to your heart, so that your mind is in your heart. As you breathe, say quietly or silently: 'Lord Jesus Christ, Son of God, have mercy on me.'"

When the pilgrim tried this kind of prayer, he found himself after a couple of days feeling lazy and burdened by the practice. He returned to the monk, who commanded the pilgrim to say the Jesus Prayer three thousand times every day.

At their next meeting, the number was increased to six thousand, then to twelve thousand. Before long the pilgrim was saying the Jesus Prayer all day, even in his sleep. His heart began praying the prayer automatically. The result was that his heart was awakened and inflamed. The pilgrim had learned a practice, and fidelity to the practice changed his life.

> Don't be afraid. Be completely in God's peace.
>
> Blessed Elizabeth of the Trinity

Our practice of prayer gives us a peek into the depths of our being, to our very source. There we are able to feel the touch of the radiance of God; there the powers of our reason and understanding fail. Those who feel the touch of God begin to enjoy and savor, rather than understand and reason. Our devotion to and our desire for the Lord take over in us, like a fire that is out of control, burning everything in its path.

After his resurrection, Jesus didn't ask for an explanation for Peter's denial. He asked instead, "Do you love me?" This question grounds contemplation. In the seasons of our life, whether tempests rage or sunrises soothe, when we are tempted to leave off our practices, perhaps feeling we no longer need them, this question, "Do you love me?" awakens us again. We seek to respond with every beat of our heart, "Yes, I love you!" This is all Jesus wants to know. It is what contemplative prayer is all about.

Creating a Rhythm

Reflect on your schedule. (You might even do this with your planner at hand.) Identify three commitments you can make for a month that would create daily space for a prayerful practice. Then identify potential obstacles, resources needed, and what would be signs of growth that would accompany keeping these commitments.

- ______________________________
- ______________________________
- ______________________________

Chapter Eighteen

Obtain Spiritual Direction

Contemplation involves not only the time we spend in prayer but every aspect of life. It challenges our choices, questions our authenticity, breaks open our life with the Spirit. We walk on new ground, uncharted territory, for no one else has gone exactly where we will go as we encounter God. And so we are blessed if we have a spiritual friend, a mentor, a spiritual director who can be our companion on the way.

It occurred to me one day that I had come to think of God much like the computer I use every day: Someone cold, someone who responded to the push of the right buttons, ran his preprogrammed processes, and definitely didn't step out from behind the screen. Whatever communication I had was actually my typing on the face of this "computer-like" God, who responded to my heart with a series of commands and drop-down menus.

One day I told this to my spiritual director. From the personal presence of my director I learned instead about a God who was always with me, giving me all of himself unceasingly, creating me in love anew at every instant.

My spiritual director patiently helped me to change my perceptions. This director walked with me, allowed me to be myself, and helped me to become who I truly wanted to be. I never felt as though I were an imposition or just another item on his "to do" list. When he was with me, there was no time. He was totally there.

Because of both the words and actions of my spiritual director, I finally came to understand what God is like.

> In your soul there is a door that leads to the contemplation of God. But you must open it.
>
> G. Bossis, *He and I*

Emmaus Road

In a way, the disciples leaving Jerusalem and walking to Emmaus were experiencing many of my misperceptions about God. They had expected a Messiah who would accomplish things their way, on their timetable, to their satisfaction. And instead, he had been killed. That was it. Their time had been wasted. Their hopes had been dashed.

Then a man caught up with them and accompanied them to their home. He was interested in their feelings about the situation. He kept them talking, while they revealed to him their fears, their disappointment, and ultimately the love that lay beneath their pain. In a sense, they were walking away from their commitment to discipleship because Jesus hadn't performed correctly (much like walking away from a computer or photocopier that doesn't perform at the push of a button).

Jesus put himself totally at their disposal for as long as they desired his presence. He taught and didn't rebuke. He listened and spoke as long as it took to ignite anew the fire in their hearts. He revealed himself in the breaking of the bread. By the time he disappeared from their midst, their commitment had been rekindled. They ran, not walked, back to Jerusalem.

What Happens in Spiritual Direction?

Spiritual direction is a conversation with another in which we share our life, our experience of prayer, the movement of the Spirit within us. As the other person listens, prays with us, and points out certain things we may not have noticed, we become more attentive and responsive to the Spirit's action in our life. He or she also helps us pay attention to God as he actively reveals himself. God's voice can be heard more clearly when the muddle of our thoughts is clarified.

A spiritual director is not a "pal," a therapist, a problem-solver, or an answer box. A spiritual director stands with us on the threshold of the sacred. He or she is a midwife who assists in the birthing of the spiritual adventure. He or she is a nurse attending the Divine Physician who heals our wounds. Thus, a spiritual director turns us gently to face the Lord. He or she deflects the efficient solution-oriented expectations fostered in us by the world in which we live. The director sits and listens, so that we learn to sit and listen both to ourselves and to God.

The spiritual direction relationship lends a type of accountability to our growth in contemplation as well as support, knowledge, and compassion. A spiritual director is a companion on the way of faith, a friend of one's soul, another self who gently and personally points out the breathings and voice of the Spirit of the Lord Jesus.

Some wonder how it is possible to allow another person into such an intimate part of one's life. How can another human person help us to discern what God is saying to us? How does opening our life to another help us to grow in freedom, in prayer, in peace?

The answers to these questions lie, perhaps, in other questions. Are you satisfied with your life, or do you sometimes wonder if there is something more? Are you content with the way you pray? Do you think there is a possibility that you are being called through contemplation to a profound encounter with God? Do you have questions about your prayer and the challenges it is offering to your life choices?

Assuming Full Responsibility

Thomas Merton, the well-known contemplative monk and spiritual director, maintained that we could only become saints by assuming full responsibility for our lives just as they are, with all their handicaps and limitations, and submitting ourselves to the purifying and transforming action of the Spirit.

Thus, upon beginning spiritual direction we may discover in ourselves obstacles to growth in a healthy relationship with God. Some of these may be a lack of personal freedom, poor self-esteem, and resistance to dealing with sinful habits. We need to confront these obstacles—even, if necessary, with the help of professional counseling—in order for spiritual direction to be as fruitful as it can be.

Throughout the journey of direction, who we are is never left behind. Instead, our identity is taken up, through self-acceptance and self-donation, into the humanity of Christ, who is forever at the right hand of the Father. The Divine Vinedresser frees us from the "burdens" that hold back our spiritual progress (see Jn 15:15). We become more securely attached like branches to Jesus the Vine, and more fully nourished by him.

> The most important thing of all to St. Paul was that he knew himself to be loved by Christ.
>
> St. John Chrysostom

Gradually, even over the course of years, we move into more distinctive spaces of Christ-life. Reflection on the Gospels draws us into their grace-filled story, so that we live only in the realm of revelation. Yet even here, the director who knows us well is able to keep us true to revelation, pointing out to us when we mistake a favorite habit or a forgotten compulsion for a graced call. A director keeps us true, helping us over hurdles that would retard us on our race for the prize of eternal encounter.

Questions to Get You Started With Your Spiritual Director

- Am I at peace? If not, what is bothering me?
- What problems am I facing? How do I react to those problems?
- Have I felt God moving me in prayer? If so, how?
- Do I have any decisions before me? If so, what do I want to do?
- Has something in my prayer stood out this past week or month, in a sense disturbing my way of life?

Choosing a Spiritual Director

It is best to look for a spiritual director who has some experience, training, and skill and who is old enough to have worked out personal hang-ups. Most of all, choose someone living an already deep prayer life, whether a priest, religious, or layperson. If no one in your area seems to have these qualifications, your diocesan Office for Spiritual Development or a local seminary or convent may offer you recommendations.

Early on, you and your spiritual director need to discuss the practical aspects of your relationship, such as your expectations, how your mentor is to be compensated, and the "initial" time period after which you and your director can assess how the relationship is going. If either of you feels that things are not working out, you should be free to say, "I don't think I want to continue with this."

On the other hand, know that spiritual growth happens in seasons. Don't walk out simply because you think someone else can help you more. Unless there is an evident reason why the relationship should be terminated, trust that it will become clear when it is time to move on. One director may be able to walk with you for a part of your journey; another may be more helpful at another time in your life.

Getting the Most Out of Spiritual Direction

Spiritual direction provides a good environment for you to reflect upon your prayer and your relationship with God. A good director helps you to focus, pointing out where the Spirit is moving in your life and where you may be offering resistance.

Other than that, the director waits, listens, and provides a place for silence and prayer. This stance teaches you to wait upon your experience, to listen for the Spirit, to welcome silence and prayer instead of efficiently coming up with strategies to resolve issues.

Ancient wisdom tells us that God gave us two ears and only one mouth because he intended us to listen more than to talk! "Listen to advice and accept instruction, that you may gain wisdom for the future" (Prv 19:20).

As we assume this childlike posture of expectant waiting, gradually we learn to relinquish control and to trust instead. It is easier to do so with another's support and example. There is no blueprint; you write the lines of your journey as you go, and the director follows your lead, patiently arousing awareness for what might be skipped over unnoticed.

> It is so good to give when one loves, and I love Him so much, this God who is jealous of having me all for himself.
>
> Blessed Elizabeth of the Trinity

The idea of facing our deepest self both threatens and entices us. The ego struggles to stay in charge, maintain control, and resist change. But the Spirit persists in asking us to change, for we need to advance until we reach the full stature of Christ. Ours is a lifetime work of growth, reconciliation, conversion, and realignment.

There is no life without death, no resurrection without the cross, no growth without conversion, no breaking through without a certain amount of breaking down. A good director knows this, and he or she facilitates the Spirit's work and your response, making sure you do not get sidetracked, fostering continual movement and growth, helping you take the next good step.

❧

Reflect on the learnings that have surfaced in this chapter. What three things do you want in your relationship with God?

- ____
- ____
- ____

In what ways do you think you would benefit from spiritual direction?

- ____
- ____
- ____

Are there any aspects of spiritual direction that make you feel concerned or anxious?

- ____
- ____
- ____

If you do not already have a spiritual director, where are some places you might begin to look for one?

- ____
- ____
- ____

Chapter Nineteen

Tell What You Have Seen

I have such a hunger for him. He hollows out abysses in my soul, abysses he alone can fill, and to do that he leads me into deep silence that I never want to leave again.

Blessed Elizabeth of the Trinity

Contemplation draws us closer and closer to the inner communication of the Trinity, deeper and deeper into the abyss of our soul. But contemplation can never bypass the humanity of Jesus, a strong theme in the writings of St. Teresa of Avila. In the person of our Lord and Master, we find access to the Trinity and come to know who we are.

The language of God is specifically tailored to each person who encounters him.

> He wants you to become a living force for all mankind, lights shining in the world. You are to be radiant lights as you stand beside Christ, the great light, bathed in the glory of him who is the light.
>
> St. Gregory Nazianzen

The apostle Thomas was missing when Jesus appeared to the apostles. He claimed that he wouldn't believe Jesus was risen until he put his hands into the wounds of the Savior. To Thomas, a man struggling with faith, Jesus spoke a very "physical" language: "Put your finger here, and see my hands; and put out your hand, and place it in my side; do not be faithless, but believe" (Jn 20:27). Jesus offered his body to Thomas so that he could touch his wounds and know that it was he.

To Mary Magdalene, on the other hand, Jesus said, "Do not hold me for I have not yet ascended to the Father" (Jn 20:17). Mary was not struggling with faith, she was shaken by love. She did not need to touch in order to confirm her faith. Love had led her beyond doubt. To one in love, Jesus instead gave a mission: "Go to my brethren and say to them ..." (Jn 20:17). Contemplation finds its fulfillment in mission.

Many whom Jesus healed, forgave, or called in the Gospels were sent to tell someone else what had been done for them. The Samaritan woman, with whom we began these pages, is one who went off to gather her whole town to hear Jesus. Those people saw for themselves, then moved on to develop their own stories of relationship to this Teacher at the well.

> Do not fear, God is with you. Be serene, joyful, happy. Carry serenity, joy, and a smile everywhere, especially where smiles are missing because God's grace is missing.
>
> Venerable Mother Thecla

The world waits for the story of what you have seen. Your contemplative living, your journeys through prayer, the crosses you have carried and shared, the nights you have passed through, God's self-revelation to you—someone is waiting to hear. Your story will be the language by which others will learn how to sit in God's presence, listen, and speak to him.

In prayer, ask God to help you call to mind the names of three persons whom you can "companion" into an experience of prayer by sharing your own journey of prayer. Write their names here:

- ____
- ____
- ____

Are there any areas of your life that you realize you still need to hand over to the Lord? What are they?

- ____
- ____
- ____

Reflect upon what aspect of your new prayer experience has been most meaningful to you:

- ____
- ____
- ____

BIBLIOGRAPHY

Allen, Joseph J. *Inner Way.* Grand Rapids, Mich.: Eerdmanns, 1994.

Barry, William A. *Allowing the Creator to Deal With the Creature.* New York: Paulist, 1994.

Brock, Sebastian, trans. *The Syriac Fathers on Prayer and the Spiritual Life.* Kalamazoo, Mich.: Cistercian, 1987.

Burrows, Ruth. *Ascent to Love.* Denville, N.J.: Dimension, 1987.

______. *Guidelines for Mystical Prayer.* Denville, N.J.: Dimension, 1976.

______. *The Cloud of Unknowing.* Edited by William Johnton. New York: Doubleday, 1973.

Congar, Yves. *I Believe in the Holy Spirit.* New York: Crossroad, 1997.

Cooper, Austin. *The Cloud.* New York: Alba, 1989.

Davies, Oliver, ed. *Rhineland Mystics.* New York: Crossroad, 1990.

de Caussade, Jean-Pierre. *The Sacrament of the Present Moment.* San Francisco: Harper & Row, 1989.

de Waal, Esther. *Seeing God.* Collegeville, Minn.: Liturgical, 1984.

del Mastro, M.L., trans. *The Revelation of Divine Love.* Liguori, Mo.: Triumph, 1994.

Dent, Barbara. *My Only Friend Is Darkness.* Notre Dame, Ind.: Ave Maria, 1988.

English, John. *Spiritual Intimacy and Community.* New York: Paulist, 1992.

Finley, James. *Merton's Palace of Nowhere.* Notre Dame, Ind.: Ave Maria, 1978.

Green, Kenneth J. *The Saturated Self.* San Francisco: Basic, 1991.

Groeschel, Benedict J. *Spiritual Passages.* New York: Crossroad, 1988.

______. *Stumbling Block and Stepping Stones.* New York: Paulist, 1987.

Hafiz. *The Subject Tonight Is Love.* N. Myrtle Beach, S.C.: Pumpkin, 1996.

Hall, Thelma. *Too Deep for Words.* New York: Paulist, 1988.

Hauser, Richard J. *Moving in the Spirit.* New York: Paulist, 1986.

Jamart, Rev. Francois. *Complete Spiritual Doctrine of St. Thérèse of Lisieux.* New York: Alba, 1961.

Johnston, William. *The Mysticism of the Cloud of Unknowing.* Trubaco Canyon, Calif.: Source, 1992.

Kabat-Zinn, Jon. *Wherever You Go There You Are.* New York: Hyperion, 1994.

Lawrence, Brother. *The Practice of the Presence of God.* Translated by Robert J. Edmonson. Orleans, Mass.: Paraclete, 1985.

Merton, Thomas. *A Thomas Merton Reader.* Edited by Thomas P. McDonnell. New York: Doubleday, 1989.

A Mirror for Souls. A French mystic of the thirteenth century. London: Gill and Macmillan, 1981.

Muto, Susan Annette. *John of the Cross for Today: The Ascent.* Notre Dame, Ind.: Ave Maria, 1991.

______. *Pathways of Spiritual Living.* Petersham, Mass: St. Bede's, 1984.

Pentkovsky, Aleksei, ed. *The Pilgrim's Tale.* New York: Paulist, 1999.

Romero, Oscar. *The Violence of Love: The Pastoral Wisdom of Archbishop Oscar Romero.* San Francisco: Harper & Row, 1988.

Salvail, Ghislaine. *At the Crossroads of the Scriptures.* Boston: Pauline, 1996.

Sheldrake, Philip, ed. *The Way of Ignatius Loyola.* St. Louis, Mo.: Institute of Jesuit Resources, 1991.

Skinner, John, ed. *Wisdom of the Cloister.* New York: Doubleday, 1999.

Turkle, Sherry. *Life on the Screen.* New York: Simon & Schuster, 1995.

Underhill, Evelyn. *Practical Mysticism.* New York: Dutton, 1943.

Urs von Balthasar, Hans. *The Moment of Christian Witness.* San Francisco: Ignatius, 1994.

______. *Unless You Become Like This Child.* San Francisco: Ignatius, 1991.

Vanier, Jean. *Community and Growth.* New York: Paulist, 1989.

von Speyr, Adrienne. *The Victory of Love.* San Francisco: Ignatius, 1990.

Wolf, Pierre. *Discernment—The Art of Choosing Well.* Liguori, Mo.: Triumph, 1993.